M000308516

ALPHA MALE
BIBLE

Charisma,
Psychology of Attraction,
Charm.
Art of Confidence,
Self-Hypnosis, Meditation.
Art of Body Language,
Eye Contact, Small Talk.
Habits & Self-Discipline
of a Real Alpha Man.

Sean Wayne

CONTENTS

Introduction

"The power of the alpha male comes from within, they don't rely upon external factors for their happiness, joy, and contentment."

— Asad Meah

Whether you're lacking confidence and self-esteem or looking to improve yourself, whether you want to work on your relationships and dating life or simply want to achieve more success, this book will essentially highlight the key aspects required for building and developing the qualities of an alpha male: A person who charms, attracts, achieves. and delivers.

You've obviously picked up the book because you've been experiencing your fair share of problems that—on the face of it—may not even seem like problems to you. Perhaps you've gotten so used to letting these problems dictate your life that you ultimately give in and plod along through life without any sense of achievement or progress. Ask yourself the following questions:

Are you shy or lacking in confidence when it comes to being around women?

Do you feel like someone who is overlooked, ignored, and disrespected, which makes it difficult for you to approach and talk to people?

Do you feel intimidated in the presence of other men with personalities that are often overpowering, stronger, and even louder?

Do you ever take a chance and go for what you want?

Except for the last question, you very likely answered yes to all of the above. And it's okay to ask these questions of yourself as it'll help you to decide if you want to stay in the state you are in or make positive, enriching, and completely transformative changes to your life and attitude that can let you change the outcomes of those questions.

In order to do so, you'll have to understand what it is that makes you what you are, and then steadily work on how to mold yourself into something different and better. You're still a work in progress no matter what state you're in, and it's never too late to work on yourself to see vast improvements. It could be something as simple as understanding the competition and finding out what women like about other guys, or determining what to do today to become a more confident and charismatic man. It could be looking deeper within yourself and remaining true to yourself, while also becoming more assertive, more self-confident, more self-disciplined.

More alpha.

Now you're probably wondering just how this book can help you achieve all that. If anything, you're probably questioning the veracity of this book and even rethinking if you'll gain anything from it at all. Perhaps you're the sort of person who needs to see a checklist of everything that will be covered and see if it contains the things that will readily affect you.

Very good, you're already showing a bit of assertiveness right now. So let's do exactly that.

1. Traits of an alpha male
2. How to be more confident and interesting
3. How to improve your appearance
4. How to communicate better

5. How to attract women and keep them interested
6. How to send a message without talking
7. How to connect with women mentally and physically
8. Practices and exercises to help you improve
9. How to improve your appearance
10. Going after your goals

See anything you like? More than one? Then you've come to the right book as you'll get in-depth knowledge and techniques that will help you become a true alpha male. You'll read from well-documented research and experience of professionals in the art of transforming yourself into a man who can not just feel good about himself, but can also make others in his orbit feel good about themselves. You will be both inspired and inspiring at the same time, and you'll hardly recognize the person you were before, relegating him to a distant memory or a bad dream.

And to achieve just that, you need to hear it from not just anyone.

You need to hear it from *Sean Wayne*.

Meet Sean Wayne

Sean Wayne is a self-made Man, graduate of International Relations and Diplomatic Science. He knows exactly what he's talking about because of his intense studies and skills in relationships of all kinds. He is an authority in personality development because to him, work, well-being, wealth, and love relationships are not just an exact science, but also a noble art. Helping people achieve the next level of being a Man matters deeply to him because what you're about to learn has helped plenty of Men gain the confidence to go after what they want. **Sean** is the perfect person to be writing this book as—thanks to his father's experience as a noted psychiatrist and his own psychophysical skills—he has become a talent, and later guru, of psychological manipulation, persuasion, and therefore... of relationships.

His goal behind writing is simply to transform anyone from any background, social upbringing, and personal beliefs into a 100% alpha male, left, right and center. And what better way to do this than getting into the psychology, habits, verbal and non-verbal language, charisma, self-esteem, vision, and a lot of tenacity of the Men who have it all, and presented by a Man who is an authority when it comes to being passionate and enthusiastic about the hows and the whys on how even you can be an ALPHA MALE. No bullshit, no snake oil; just pure, hard facts that you may never have realized until you picked up this book.

Above all else, the goal of **Sean Wayne** while letting you in on this Bible full of secrets and strategies is simply to let you reach the pinnacle of your potential as a Man. His love for the topic and willingness to share it with anyone who can benefit from this for the better is a testament to just how much he wishes for everyone to resolve their deep-seated pains and inadequacies, and have the opportunity to finally achieve the absolute pleasure they could only dream of. Living the reality of a real ALPHA MALE.

Chapter 1

The Alpha Male

If you've already picked up this book, there's a high probability you did so because you felt it's missing from your life. The cover, the subtitle, the magnetism of the image that's formed in your head all told you that this is what you need right now.

And looking at the book is just the trigger. You see it happening all around you on social media, in the movies, on red carpet events, and even at that upscale restaurant you've only heard about but never even considered going to. You've seen them stepping out of their cars and it's as if the world automatically switches over to slow motion. The camera flashes sparkle and gleam all around and the sounds of adulation and cheers surround the area, all focused on the one person who commands it all.

Just what is it that's so attractive about them? Is it the persona, the look, the subtle charm that you know is there, but they won't show it right away until the time is right? They command the modern-day jungle like an apex predator, gracefully and carefully scanning everyone and anyone, finding their next kill.

You know who they are. You know just what they're capable of. But more importantly, you know you're not one of them.

Not yet, anyway.

Beta Male Traits that Make You Unattractive

You might be wondering how it could have happened. How you, someone pleasant and possibly affable, could be where you are right now instead of being one of the distinguished few. The fact that you're not an alpha male yourself isn't just a case of not being at the right place at the right time. It takes dedication, strength of will, perseverance, and of course, an attitude that does not relent. An alpha male recognizes the potential of his very existence and uses every weapon in his arsenal to make things happen for him and him alone. And the first thing they recognize is this: They are second to none.

In short, to be the alpha, you need to stop being the beta.

This is where the lessons you learned your whole life might be spinning around in your head. "Slow and steady wins the race," "play it safe," "take no chances," etc. are some of the idioms you grew up with and may have been what kept your ambitions in check. It does sound like the ideal solution to lead a simple and mundane existence without taking any risks and getting out of your comfort zone. And sure, if that's what appeals to you, by all means look forward to that drive back to your apartment and having leftovers for your TV dinner. Don't forget to put the book back where you picked it up from. You won't be needing it after all.

Still here? Good. That means you've decided to take the plunge. And in order to do that, you need to understand just what it is that's holding you back.

The Need for Approval

Being a beta sounds simple enough. Looking up to a role model whose life moves at a pace you can't ever imagine yourself in will undoubtedly leave you in awe. Of course, the need to please can be a driving force for almost every aspect of life. From being a teacher's pet to the good son who does no wrong, to even being the model employee who understands his place on the organizational chart, life as a beta sounds like a monotonous and run-of-the-mill existence that one could be content with from the cradle to the grave. But let's face it, you really can't call this living, can you? Not without having done anything even remotely exciting in your entire life.

And if that realization is lighting a fire inside you, then good news: There's hope for you yet. But only if you understand that your secondary role as a beta isn't doing you any favors. The fact that you live for the approval of others only elevates their position in contrast to your own and makes you nothing more than a yes-man who would rather keep others happy at your own expense. You would like nothing more than to be the nice guy everyone can count on to take one for the team whenever the chips are down, or to put in extra hours whenever a deadline starts looming. That's who you are: Mr. Dependable. Never saying no, never forming your own opinion, and going with the flow have turned you tame and timid.

You may think you have your own reasons for doing so. Perhaps you're the kind of guy who doesn't want to antagonize. Perhaps you're the person who wants to be liked by everyone and hated by no one. Perhaps you'd rather not get into an argument over the smallest minutiae of existence if only if you could avoid creating a hassle. But once you start putting others before yourself, you automatically disintegrate your own position not just in your mind, but in the minds of everyone else around you. You may think volunteering for extra shifts makes you some kind of hero. In reality, everyone's relieved it isn't them—which means they've got more going on with their lives, and that should worry you a great deal.

Keeping Score

You give and you give with the expectation that sooner or later you can expect the others to respect you for your aid. This isn't an unreasonable expectation. Doing something for others in order to be more of a gentleman and swooping in to save the day from total disaster is one thing, but it's another thing entirely to devote all your effort and energy with the sole expectation that it will all be reciprocated. If you haven't understood by now, everyone looks out for number one. And if you're doing all these favors under the impression that sooner or later you can call on anyone to bail you out of a pickle, well, tough luck (*What Is A Beta Male?*, n.d.).

There's a reason why everyone can count on you to be there when they need help: Because you'll never say no. On the other hand, they'll only ask you to cover for them or take care of the tasks they'd rather not do because they are the kind of people who would say no. While you're there with a feeling of satisfaction over helping a fellow man, they've already forgotten about it. Out of sight, out of mind.

Shirking From Taking Charge

Being in the beta position makes one more subservient to a dominant force. With the way a beta is wired, their attitude doesn't offer much in terms of taking chances and becoming a figure one can look up to. This makes a beta far more prone to being a follower and never a leader. Leading would be the antithesis of their being, since it would put them in a spot that requires being decisive, efficient, commanding, and most important of all, inspiring. Stepping up to the task and rising to the occasion comes as second nature to an alpha, which leaves all the betas in his wake ready to follow him.

This is where you—as a beta—find yourself. You'd rather be a follower and ride on an alpha's coattails, but that is pretty much all you'll be able to do. It could be because of the need for approval, or for not causing any kind of antagonism among your peers. Worse still, you may have zero confidence in your own abilities as you've never really considered yourself to be a problem solver. Nevertheless, until you break the cycle of being subservient and dependent on someone else for guidance and direction, your chances of being your own man are extremely limited. This will always keep you second-guessing yourself and never even imagining yourself in a position where you could lead others effectively and efficiently.

Submissive Body Language

Any attitude, whether alpha or beta, reflects on your outward appearance. Your sense of attire and the way you carry it offers a visual representation of your place in the pecking order, and nowhere is this more obvious than in the way you move. Your body language conveys a great deal about your mindset. The simplest impression of one's posture can tell you just where that person considers themselves, with an upright and confident stance oozing a sense of charisma and self-assuredness.

On the other hand, a weak and submissive stance where one is slouching, drooping shoulders, or looks just uninterested shows that their attitude is terribly defeatist. It's as if they woke up this morning with a ton of regrets and continue to carry it everywhere they go. This is not the kind of person you can count on to step up to the plate when the going gets tough. This isn't the kind of man you can rely on in a situation where taking risks becomes mandatory. And this certainly isn't the man who can inspire others to follow his example.

Thus your stance and body language are the first and foremost indicators of whether or not you're an alpha. To make matters worse, it takes very little time for anyone to figure out that you're a beta from a defeatist body language, making you someone who is afraid to take risks, lacks confidence, and has a pessimistic and submissive attitude to go along with it (Loki, 2011).

Do You Have These Qualities?

Of course you do! You wouldn't be here otherwise. Life as a beta becomes your standard operating procedure, which leaves very little room for spicing things up a bit. And the simple fact is that there are betas everywhere you look, which makes your chances of standing out virtually nonexistent. So far, you've seen just how much this can be a turn-off for other people. Alphas will only let you hang around them because they know how much you need this chance. But other betas will consider you nothing special, since they don't have enough self-worth as it is to even recognize a peer. Your immediate social circle both at work and home will come to see you as an average Joe who's there to fill up the numbers, but that's about it. With that kind of position in the pecking order, a romantic liaison is going to be the furthest thing from your mind. For one thing, you're certainly not carrying any of the excitement women crave for. For another, your lack of confidence and self-esteem won't even get you a few feet close to women. They would most likely see you coming from a mile away and just turn their face away in disgust (PC, 2018).

Consequences of Not Being an Alpha Male

Lack of Attraction

An alpha male is a unique commodity. In a world where betas swarm to gain any kind of attention, alphas shine like diamonds in the rough, which makes them immediately alluring. Their raw charm and magnetism are more than enough to be sought after by practically every woman in the room. But as a beta, you may as well not even be alive, let alone in the same room.

Though your own natural looks may not be to everyone's liking, they can be worked on. Like a stone that is chipped and chiseled to form a majestic sculpture, the rough edges around a beta are just there to be chipped off to form something a lot more attractive and appealing. But in the absence of any self-worth, that puts most betas out of the running for any kind of woman. They seek something wild and adventurous, and your basic appearance with virtually no grooming doesn't make you any different from the guy who rings up their purchases at a checkout counter.

Nervousness and Anxiety

A lack of self-confidence and a general relegation to the position of being a beta makes one far less audacious. This is a surefire way to be completely unprepared for any kind of social situations, let alone those which may lead to romantic liaisons. Much like how it happens in the movies, women do prefer men to be assertive enough to hold a fascinating conversation with them or be completely at ease in their presence. An alpha can create those ideal circumstances just by their energy and charisma where women find themselves drawn in and not wanting to leave. But with a beta, women can sense their level of anxiety just from the way they start to speak or avoid eye contact. Even if you manage to strike up a conversation, it's only a matter of time before you can no longer hold their attention.

And that's only when you actually make your move. More often than not, betas may not even get that far. Instead, they will avoid the inevitable fear of rejection and embarrassment by simply passing up another opportunity to meet someone interesting. "Nothing ventured, nothing gained."

Lack of Self-Esteem

The most crucial environment any man needs to master is at work. Being noticed by colleagues, peers and managers at your place of business where you're bound to spend about sixty to seventy percent of your day means maintaining a certain social image that puts you at a particular position of respect and prestige. And while having a positive and upbeat attitude helps to create a kind of popularity, having a natural charisma, flair and assertiveness creates an aura, an attraction, and even a mystery. It makes people look up their workstations and take notice whenever they get a whiff of your unique perfume and hear the distinct taps of your designer shoes approaching their way.

But in the case of a beta, who by definition is far from being a social animal, is usually relegated to a place of irrelevance. The beta doesn't create any kind of stir to have friends that can elevate his self-esteem in any way. Aside from other betas, your chances at being asked out to drinks after work or checking out the brand new restaurant downtown in the company of friends are essentially zero. This is even after you go out of your way to be helpful and nice, which we've already looked at above. More often than not, being precluded from such social gatherings also takes you out of the notice of your immediate managers or supervisors, who love seeing teams functioning well both at work and out of it.

This can paint you as not a team player, or someone who would rather not be included in office events such as corporate retreats, picnics, and beach excursions.

Your shy attitude limits your potential to grow out of your shell and portrays you as a non-starter to management, who would love to see the most dynamic and energetic people at the forefront of their company. Ultimately, you'll be overlooked for promotions every year and have fewer friends at work, aside from other betas, who are pretty much negligible.

Thus your beta attitude leads to your own downfall and leaves you as nothing more than a barely noticed piece of furniture (Bacon, n.d.-b).

Essential Traits of an Alpha Male

Let's get something out of the way first: You don't have to be an asshole to be an alpha male. Sure, they have the swagger, the physique, the attitude that makes sliced bread a relic, but that doesn't mean they harbor any malice toward others, particularly non-alphas.

Naturally, they didn't get to where they are just by playing by the rules. They set their own path and walked under no one's direction unless it meant getting to their desired goals. They understand full well what they want out of life, and it's nothing less than everything they can set their minds to. Fast cars, luxurious properties, bodies sculpted out of marble, their pick of any and all women in their field of vision, and of course, to be the face that has everyone's attention—there are virtually no limits to their ambition. So they're not going to be too nice about all that they've achieved and, to a beta, they may as well be the Greek gods of old.

And that suits the alphas just fine.

Assertive and Persuasive

An alpha has successfully mastered the art of having an assertive attitude and excellent communication skills that go hand in hand. They're fully aware of their surroundings, like kings of the jungle, and are content with the knowledge that they are masters of their domain. It requires patience, self-assuredness, and persistence to achieve their goals. To them, everything is a potential challenge that only they can accomplish. A successful career, independent wealth, the awe of their social circles, and the company of good women; nothing is off-limits. And like we saw earlier, they have no qualms about breaking the rules to get it all. In fact, they set the pace. They make the rules. Everyone else is just along for the ride. In short, the alpha knows his place at the top. He has clearly set goals about what he wants to achieve out of his life and is willing to do absolutely anything and everything it takes to do so.

With an attitude that exudes confidence and assertiveness, an alpha will never shy away from speaking his mind. He will remain unapologetic as he owns his desires without any sense of shame or guilt. If it means achieving what he wants out of his life, he will make sure to say so as clearly and confidently as possible. With a strong mastery of communication skills, an alpha uses class, charm, and respect to be incredibly persuasive in order to get what he wants, and also ensures that the give and take is enough to not just work to his advantage, but also to remain fair to an extent with the other party. It is vitally important for the alpha to leave the other party with a sense of dignity and respect while extracting his own needs from them.

This is why an alpha is not essentially an asshole. Nevertheless, he sets clear boundaries with everyone he deals with and speaks up emphatically when he is crossed (Andrew Ferebee, 2019a).

A Gentleman to the Core

By definition, an alpha male espouses all the qualities of a gentleman: He is courteous, polite and considerate. Even though he prioritizes his own well-being, he genuinely cares about the needs of the people in his life and wants the best for others. There is nothing untoward in his intentions, nor is there any malice. His success depends on whether or not his associations consider him to be fair and likeable, though he doesn't necessarily require any validation from them. Instead, he would rather form a genuine connection with his peers and the people who come to love and adore him. His positive attitude and fun-loving nature makes being in his life a privilege, and it is one that people treasure. Being in his orbit is a fulfillment unlike any other, and the alpha will ensure it offers more value to everyone. Sharing positive emotions, having fun around the town, and enjoying life to the fullest is always on his agenda.

Able to Trust Himself

Even with a coterie of friends and well-wishers who want nothing more than what's best for him, an alpha will always be self-reliant when it matters the most. While he welcomes any advice or help whenever need be, he knows that the most important decisions always come down to him. This is because he is capable of trusting his own judgment and knows that any major decisions must be taken by him and him alone.

It also allows him to keep track of the areas he may consider himself to be vulnerable. When he finds himself out of his depth, he can identify the need to seek appropriate counsel. It is an acknowledgement of his own areas of improvement when faced with a situation he isn't able to successfully navigate. He can then be the bigger man, admit his own ignorance in the matter, and seek out the help and guidance of those he can trust as much as he trusts himself.

Most importantly, an alpha relies on his own judgment to take full responsibility for his actions and their outcomes. Whatever the outcomes might be, the alpha will either change them or accept them until he is able to use them to his advantage. He will never complain about unfairness and being given the short end of the stick. All his decisions are on him and him alone, and thus he won't start blaming others for any misfortunes (*Top 5 Traits of a Confident Alpha Male | Manscaped.com*, 2018).

Self-Evolution and Mastery

An alpha male does not limit himself to his present circumstances. His drive and hunger to continuously grow and evolve push him toward bettering and renewing his circumstances every day. It's not enough to remain resting on his laurels. To an alpha, every day brings new possibilities and challenges that he must master.

This ambition and drive for growth and mastery also curtail any and all lingering self-doubt an alpha may have. Being human, after all, an alpha also has his own fair share of demons to deal with, and it is essential to be able to tackle these inner demons head-on. These nagging voices of self-doubt still reside in his head, and it is a constant battle for an alpha to wrestle them into submission and assert complete control over his life and fate.

An alpha also continues to learn from each experience and encounter, even if they do not work in his favor. Such lessons are important in maintaining a sense of humility in themselves which keeps them grounded enough to move on from one challenge to the next. Any unfavorable outcomes serve as a lesson for alphas to adapt and learn in order to have a different outcome whenever such a challenge poses itself again. Thus it is certainly possible to use active learning to not just become an alpha male, but also to be a better one every day.

Chapter 2

It All Starts from Within

One thing you'll have to understand is this: No one becomes an alpha male by someone holding your hand and taking you through the ropes. It requires patience, hard work, dedication, and above all else, self-belief. Being an alpha male isn't just a skill set that comes with a diploma. It is a mindset, an attitude, a lifestyle that remains a part of you whether you're awake or not. Believing that you can be an alpha male, despite all your failings and any and all beta qualities that you may have, is the first step toward realizing your goals. It is also worth understanding that not every alpha male is born as one. Even they've had to make sacrifices in order to realize their goals and become the best versions of themselves, and the first step toward that is recognizing their potential from within. That is what you'll have to do if you want to be an alpha male: You must first start to think and feel like one.

Self-Acceptance

Understanding who you are and what makes you tick puts you on the road for transformation to an alpha male. Remember that an alpha male recognizes his own potential while at the same time accepting his own failings and determining ways to resolve them. It's part of his self-evolution to continue to improve upon his design. Therefore, accepting who you are and what you're capable of is essential to position yourself in the true alpha-male mindset. At its most basic form, this mindset is all about being comfortable, at peace, and confident in who you are.

Unconditional and Liberating

Accepting your own failings is a learning and realization experience. They are in no way there to limit your understanding or your potential. Identifying your flaws and failings allows you to decide the best way to deal with them and overcome them in order to become an alpha male. Nevertheless, it's possible that they may overwhelm you to think that this goal is beyond your reach. But this is an assumption that you cannot fall for if you want to become an alpha male. Identifying these weaknesses is one thing, but they are not the be-all and end-all of your existence. They do not drive you or motivate you. If anything, they keep you stagnant and floundering in a beta existence.

Use these weaknesses or limitations to your advantage instead of making them your defining characteristics. Any flaw is there to be overcome much like any other challenge, and the sooner you accept that, the better. Having this awareness does not interfere with our ability to fully accept ourselves in any way. And utilizing this self-awareness helps you to be true to yourself about who you are and not just who you want to be, but also who you don't want to be (Seltzer, 2008).

Being Kinder to Yourself

Recognizing your own faults and failings is one thing, but that doesn't mean you have to be overly critical about them. Circumstances in life may have brought you along a path that has left your full potential unrealized, so it isn't something that you should beat yourself up about. Rather, these are all opportunities that require your understanding and a complete game plan. The first step on the road to accepting who you are is to be compassionate to the person you've been all this time. Understand that the circumstances that made you who you are have become irrelevant now that you're looking to change. Forget the past and focus on the alpha male you want to be in the near future (Rezzan Huseyin, 2018).

Developing self-compassion allows you to love yourself as a person, no matter what version of it you are. That's why this is the logical starting point of your journey to become an alpha male: Only by loving and caring for yourself can you build on changing your mindset and working on your shortcomings. Only by loving yourself do you realize that there's so much more you can do for yourself. If you really want to be pampered and spoiled and made to feel like you're special, who better to do it first than yourself?

Transforming your Mindset

It's only logical that, as you begin to change your mindset from a beta to an alpha male, you begin to not just think but also behave differently than you did before. As an alpha male, you will start putting yourself first and seek out opportunities that benefit you the most, while also taking into consideration the people who will come to be in awe of you. This transformation is going to make your previous habits, opinions, preferences, and orientations a thing of the distant past, and you won't be able to recognize the person you were before. As you've seen in the previous chapter, your ability to trust yourself and continuously grow will create a brand-new you each and every time you wake up in the morning (Antony, 2016).

A Growth-Oriented Mindset

An alpha male is a constantly evolving creature. He must keep up with the times and the trends, not to mention learning from any and all setbacks. For all the confidence and self-belief an alpha may have, there can and will be times when he may not get his way. This is not an unprecedented scenario and is to be expected in such a dynamic world the alpha is a part of. Remember that he isn't perfect and neither are you, so there will be times when you aren't successful in a certain endeavor. This should be taken as an opportunity to learn and grow. If an alpha male stumbles, they do their best to straighten up and not fall. Only from such failures can an alpha male truly keep growing (Davis, 2019).

There will also be times when an alpha male may also seek guidance and feedback regarding any shortcomings. Feedback is also vital in the cycle of growth, and alphas are quite gracious in being a part of someone else's self-growth. It's a humbling exercise for them, and it provides them insights into your approach as well. Why? Because they might learn something, too. It's a give-and-take unlike any other in which healthy and positive feedback from each other makes both of you better than you were before.

Moving to a growth-oriented mindset will also be a sharp contrast to your earlier mindset, which was fixed and limiting and kept you from understanding all things you could accomplish. All this requires is a dedicated effort and a healthy and positive attitude.

The Alpha Don'ts

As an alpha male, it is vital to understand the kind of character you'll be emulating and the person everyone will see you as. What people will definitely not enjoy seeing is someone who constantly complains or whines, whether it's about the littlest of things such as your dinner being cold or your name not being in the guest list. An alpha must take things in his stride and always maintain composure. This allows him to determine an appropriate solution instead of complaining. Similarly, an alpha male will never set the blame on someone else's shoulders out of frustration. This behavior carries on from complaining, wherein you may find another outlet to take on the blame for something that should be in your control. Making excuses for such events paints you in a negative light among your peers and also shows you as someone who isn't completely self-assured. That is certainly not a picture you want to paint for yourself as an alpha male.

Also, alpha males should not overthink a situation and refuse to move on from any setbacks. In order to constantly evolve, the alpha-male mindset has no room for overthinking or feeling self-conscious, and should refrain from seeking approval from others. This can only lead to a negative mindset, which can be easily avoided.

The Alpha Dos

Conversely, being an alpha male is all about being in control of the situation. Self-belief and self-reliance are what drive you toward finding your purpose and not just pursuing it, but attaining it. Once you realize the power that you have, you'll be able to face your fears and be ready to take on any and all challenges that come your way—which, as an alpha, will be plenty. Conflicts can and do arise from time to time, especially when they lie in the path of your goals.

Furthermore, your ambitious drive will open you to criticism from all quarters, particularly from people who feel threatened by your energy. Nevertheless, it's important to understand that some criticism may actually be valid, especially if anything you say or do causes genuine grief to someone who may not deserve it. Therefore, be receptive to criticism and process it to determine if any of it could be a failing to work on. Above all else, believe in yourself to know that you're a bigger person for acknowledging your own imperfections, and also embracing them to become better over time. Embracing such imperfections chisels off the layers you don't need and helps you find your purpose, which is important if you want to get ahead. It also helps you to critically evaluate your key strengths and explore the areas you need to work on in order to overcome your weaknesses. This will take time and dedication, so rushing through is not recommended. Trust the process and value it, as the process itself is worth more than the end result.

Building Mental Resilience and Toughness

The American Psychological Association (APA) (2012) defines mental resilience as "being able to adapt well in the face of adversity, trauma, tragedy, threats or significant sources of threats." Over the course of your existence, your mental state must have undergone several stages of development, which no doubt came from facing certain threats to your mental and emotional stability. But often, you may fail to realize what certain mental trauma does to you and it begins to become a part of your existence without you even knowing it. You may lose sight of the way you fall into emotions and become prone to outbursts as well as retreating into yourself without actually facing the trauma. This stifles your ability to grow out of your shell and keeps you at the beta stage.

Identifying Negativity

To put yourself on the path to achieve mental toughness, you must decide on taking notice of all that is going through your mind. That means taking an unfiltered look at all the thoughts and perceptions you experience, whether positive or negative. The key here is to make sure that you remain receptive to the thoughts that do not demotivate or demoralize you, while at the same time do your best to avoid latching on to the negativity that is prevailing in your life. Otherwise, negativity has a way of overwhelming your very self and you'll end up identifying personally with those thoughts or feelings.

Being an alpha male means being able to control the emotions that may seek to overwhelm you and take your eyes off your goals. Healthy emotions such as love and joy make you feel more positive and energetic, whereas negative emotions such as anger, hate, and jealousy only lead you to resent not just other people, but also yourself. Moreover, a positive emotional outlook makes you commit to your goal more readily and helps you to be more driven as a person and ready to accept new challenges with hope and optimism. This way, you're more trusting of your own abilities while also recognizing any shortcomings, and you're ready to work on them to adapt to any new changes that come your way.

Steps to Develop Mental Resilience and Toughness

As you saw above, positive thinking is at the root of developing mental resilience. Not being weighed down by the negativity and focusing on the positives make you tougher in the face of new challenges and also helps you to manage your own anxiety. Visualizing where you want to be in the future and setting your own goals accordingly create a path on which you can become an alpha male in the truest sense, and keeping your attention on these goals makes sure you aren't distracted from your true purpose by the threats and forces that only negate your self-worth and keep you forever stuck in a beta existence (Ribeiro, 2019).

The Art of Confidence

An alpha male is more than the sum of his good looks and exquisite grooming. It takes a certain attitude and level of confidence that appeals to people and makes him instantly attractive. Confidence in an alpha male is essential in order to draw in everyone without making them feel threatened. It relaxes people and makes them feel like the alpha male values them greatly, thus gaining their attention solely on him.

Personally, confidence gives you the ability to reduce any and all fear and anxiety within you, provides greater motivation to be your best self, makes you more resilient, and fosters deeper connections and improved relationships. Confidence also makes you more willing to try new things and engage in new experiences, not to mention stops you from second-guessing yourself and makes you ready to form new connections. You also won't worry about what people think of you or ever feel the need to compare yourself with others (Harbinger, 2014).

Building Confidence

In order to become a more confident version of yourself and remain at ease with what others perceive about you, you must first stop drawing comparisons with other people. You're a unique individual and comparing yourself with others only creates an environment of negativity, which isn't good for your confidence at all. Believe in yourself and look at what you've already achieved on your road to becoming an alpha male, as it has taken so much effort on your part. Remember the things that you're good at and keep reminding yourself of your merits. By that, we do mean actually verbally reminding yourself. No one can do a better job of motivating you than yourself, and you know exactly what to say to get you in the right frame of mind. It has to be all positive, though, which means that negative self-talk is absolutely not allowed (Morin, 2019).

Don't forget that you're not prone to flaws, so you can actually do more to change your present state. Start with your mind, as like other things, being an alpha male is als a state of mind. If you tell yourself what you are and what you're capable of, your mind will believe you and create the right ideas for you to believe in. It already believes you when you doubt yourself and fill yourself with negativity. Therefore, you need to depart from the negative reinforcement and focus more on building yourself up. Visualize the ideal version of yourself that you want to be and work on it to achieve that version. Learn new skills, make subtle changes to your appearance and attire, and even seek out advice from friends, peers, and also professionals. Building a firm support group of all of these people reminds you that you're not alone and there are many people there who believe in you.

Above all else: Don't just think, act! Taking action at the right time builds and enhances your confidence.

Confidence Is a State of Mind

Being more confident starts with you. Your mind believes exactly what you tell it, and you'll tell it exactly what you believe. Therefore, your belief in yourself has to be firm and resolute, which is how you'll be able to motivate your mind to act. You're the hero of your story, and so it has to be one where you are the master of your own destiny. It certainly can't be one where you aren't confident or continue to harbor any self-doubts. It's a continuous cycle where your confidence fuels your positivity and your positivity fuels your confidence, which means that neither of them can fall to self-doubt (Kennedy, 2018).

The Role of Meditation

A great way to strengthen your mind to think positively and develop a healthy attitude is mindfulness meditation. It is about being truly present in the moment, letting your thoughts come and go, and allowing yourself to be aware of those incoming thoughts while observing them nonjudgmentally.

There are two very specific ways that meditation can help you to transform a lack of self-esteem into inner confidence, self-acceptance, and self-belief. Firstly, meditation enables you to meet and greet the person you are, and gradually become friends with that person. Once you begin to understand the kind of person you are and the things that you believe in, the next step makes it easier to bring acceptance and loving kindness to all aspects of yourself.

Surprisingly, you may even uncover a deeper belief that you do not deserve to be happy or that you aren't good enough, much like an unconscious built-in self-destruct sequence. But meditation can help you shed the light of kindness upon that self-negation and lack of self-esteem until such uncertainty dissolves into love (J. D. Moore, 2017).

Other Benefits of Meditation

Aside from discovering your true self and learning to love it even more, meditation yields certain other benefits that you may not even immediately notice. It improves your overall sense of well-being and makes you more in tune with your own needs and sustenance. It makes you in charge of your emotions and helps you to regulate your emotions, which in turn reduces any tendencies to being emotionally reactive. This way, you're less stressed and clear-headed enough to be more focused and insightful about the things around you and even yourself.

Meditating Effectively

Whether it's something as simple as breathing deeply or as complex as repeating a mantra in your mind, the ultimate goal of meditation is to create a calm and soothing atmosphere to allow your mind to quiet down from all thoughts. Relaxation exercises such as nature excursions, meditation for focused attention or loving-kindness, mindfulness and self-awareness meditation, transcendental meditation such as zen, and yoga can also channel your thoughts positively and help you clearly focus your mind on your goals.

Using Self-Hypnosis

Another unique method of getting yourself into the ideal alpha-male mindset is a technique called self-hypnosis. It isn't commonly recommended for generally reinforcing positive mindsets, but self-hypnosis is a great means of learning how to focus and motivate yourself and becoming more self-aware. It allows you to realize your full potential and make the best use of your innate skills as you learn to have better control of your thoughts and reactions while enjoying the physical and emotional benefits of the relaxation, which is typical of self-hypnosis techniques. Thus it can be a truly empowering practice (Yapko, 2020).

More Goal-Focused than Meditation

While the end result of both meditation and self-hypnosis is to promote physical and mental health, they do so in parallel ways. This highlights the merits of learning to develop and use focus meaningfully, so self-hypnosis can achieve better results if you are setting your mind to achieve specific goals.

Improve Confidence and Self-Esteem

The first thing that you'll have to decide is a goal or intention that you hope to achieve from self-hypnosis. You could wish to control a certain aspect of your life or to change your circumstances when it comes to loving yourself or having a higher level of self-confidence. Then, create a statement that embodies these characteristics that should be simple and easy to repeat in less than five seconds. Be in a comfortable position as you do this and inhale gently with deep, calculated breaths. Count the amount of seconds while you inhale and hold for half that time, then exhale for the same number of seconds that you inhaled until it becomes natural and automatic. Visualize your breaths traveling to your core, then speak your goal. Say it as if it were happening right in front of you and that you've achieved it. Smile and appreciate the fact that you have achieved this goal and don't shy away from expressing your gratitude verbally (Karp, 2015).

Chapter 3

Catching Their Eye

An alpha male is in complete control of his environment. He sets the pace and the tone, and is a natural head-turner in any social situation. Alphas ooze charm, charisma, and raw sexual appeal, which makes them attractive in so many different ways. And they've certainly mastered the art of being the only one in the room who gathers all the attention for all the right reasons.

This is their standard operating setting: To attract. They rarely need to seek out the attention of anyone, particularly the ladies. This could put them at a disadvantage, and that's not a situation you want to find yourself in. Therefore, you'll need to understand the fundamentals of the psychology of attraction.

Psychology of Attraction

Attraction works in several different ways, and the chances of being noticed increase significantly if you possess more than one attribute that makes you attractive. Whether people care to admit it or not, many of them are drawn to the outward appearance first, as it is the easiest first box on a checklist of attraction. Men and women both tend to take others at face value before digging deeper into the rest of the person. Thus an outward aesthetic appeal acts as a key to a deeper chamber.

Human attraction, on the other hand, is far more complex than it appears at first sight. While the outward appearance draws first glances, the subtlety and effort with which it is presented tends to show a careful and deliberate approach toward everything the alpha male does. The way he dresses, the products he uses on his hair or skin, and the manner with which he carries it all show a deeper level of confidence, sophistication, self-assuredness, and strength of character. This makes human attraction a far more important attribute than the physical one.

There are universal standards of attraction that are not skin deep, but rather fundamentally anchored in adaptive problems that have to be solved in mate selection, regardless of whether you're male or female. Women tend to be drawn to physical characteristics that indicate good health, mental grooming, and a likely ability to provide and protect. These characteristics could include having broad shoulders with narrower hips, a well-toned and athletic frame, a strong jawline, and a deep voice. It automatically shows the man's level of self-discipline and overall appeal that women find to be attractive qualities. Nevertheless, not having all these physical qualities isn't the end of the road. There are other central elements of romantic attraction, in fact three, that make you a highly sought-after commodity (Dawson, 2020).

Physical Attractiveness

You've seen above how your outward appearance is always the first thing to be noticed. This isn't just a superficial tendency, but also has deeper reasons. Physical features that tend to be the most attractive to others are the ones that serve as the best indicators of health and fitness. Because these features can change with our health over time, however, the most attractive features are those most under our control to manage, too. Things like proper grooming and basic physical fitness, then, may be more important than having the perfect chest or the most symmetrical nose.

In a study by Mehrabian and Blum (1997), the most attractive quality in a person came down to self-care. This showed a personal commitment to being the best a person could be. The most attractive features include a good and upright posture that exudes confidence, noticeable grooming that highlights sophistication and attention to detail over each and every aspect of your appearance, well-tailored and bespoke clothing made of the finest materials and made to showcase you in the perfect light, a seemingly positive attitude, and a reasonably healthy weight. All of the above qualities help those who do not have the perfect physique, and clothing and grooming plays a crucial role in physical attraction.

Psychological Attractiveness

While the physical features form an initial spark of attraction, an alpha male can also use his own innate psychological qualities to create a deeper and more substantial attraction. Attracting someone psychologically shows an alpha male's abilities as well as motivations for forming relationships and connections that are more long-term and emotionally intimate. Such attractiveness is usually displayed through a pleasant and cheerful personality which puts the others at ease and even brings out the best in them. It shows an inherently friendly and communal nature that strives to form a sense of harmony and comfort among peers and in one's self. Developing psychological attractiveness involves learning new skills that will help in developing rapport with anyone and everyone around you.

Behavioral Attractiveness

Though physical and psychological attractiveness can form anyone's opinions positively about an alpha male to a certain extent, it is also pertinent to mention that a more obvious indicator that creates instant appeal is the way the alpha male behaves and acts. Behavioral attractiveness shows a strength of will and certainty which makes them a lot more appealing and desirable for everyone around them. This can include anything from an engaging use of body language and hand gestures to the way you smile and look at the people in your orbit, not to mention the way you engage with other people not immediately in your circle. For instance, dealing with the wait staff at a restaurant, or casually patting the parking valet on the shoulder for a job well done shows your level of empathy, and such behavior goes a long way for everyone to take notice of you as a suave and charming personality that takes pride in any and all connections that you form.

Why Appearances Matter

It may sound like a rather shallow and superficial concept, but an unquestionable quality of an alpha male is to put careful and considered effort into his outward appearance. Much like any of the other possessions such as a car, home, and accessories, an alpha male invests greatly in the way he looks and dresses not just to make himself more physically attractive, but also because he holds himself to a much higher standard. Putting yourself first isn't a crime, and going all out to making yourself appear a lot more attractive and good-looking is an indicator of having a positive opinion of yourself. You might think this makes you more glib or insecure, but looks do matter a lot. Just not the way you might be thinking (Smith, 2018).

Indication of Self-Respect

If you truly value yourself as a person and a human being, would you think too little of yourself to not make an effort in the way you look? Being in love with the person you are means treating and pampering yourself to the finer things in life, and how you look says a lot to everyone about who you are and how you feel about yourself. Staying physically fit, being well-groomed, and dressing appropriately are indications that you respect and feel good about yourself, and therefore want to present yourself in the best way possible. A positive and healthy self-image is essential to make yourself feel like a million dollars, therefore making you more attractive not just physically, but as someone who loves and cares for themselves a great deal. It is that kind of positive self-presentation that attracts everyone instantly and makes them want to know you more.

Look, Feel, and Be Healthy

Hitting the gym regularly, watching what you eat, and engaging yourself in physically thrilling activities such as outdoor sports, hiking, swimming, etc. creates an aura of adventure and free-spiritedness about you in the eyes of others. Not only does it make you a fit and well-shaped physical specimen, but being adventurous in your activities gives you a zest for life and prepares you to take on new challenges. This contributes not just to your physical health, but also your mental and emotional health. Naturally, looking like you work out regularly rather than sitting on a couch would be an instant turn-on for most women, but looking at your active lifestyle as well as keen interest and enthusiasm in such activities is an even bigger turn-on.

Sexual Attraction

With such vigor and enthusiasm for different activities that challenge you physically and mentally, you become a stronger person in women's eyes as well as their minds. They find your lust for life and perfection to be lustful, for a lack of a better word, and begin yearning for that kind of attention. Knowing that you value yourself and your body quite highly, they cannot wait to receive similar treatment. They would love to see just how tender and respectful you can be to their needs, and that in turn lights up the spark of sexual interest within them for you.

Self-Esteem

It is almost always true that when you feel like you look good, you feel better about yourself. You tend to stand a little taller when you feel like you are the most attractive version of yourself. This in turn projects outwards in the manner you carry yourself in public, and your immediate company can get an idea of your own self-esteem as well. Plus it is actually helpful that others think more in superficial terms than they should and are instantly attracted to your well-groomed physical appearance. This doesn't just apply to intimate connections with women. Even among your friends and peers, your appearance exudes enough confidence for them to trust you with having the solution to any and all of the problems they might have. They begin to look up to you as a paragon of intelligence and dependability. It may even work in your favor when your immediate managers notice the effort you put in your outward appearance. Being well-dressed, well-groomed, and physically fit shows the level of dedication you have to all aspects of your life, including your work. People who invest in their appearance more are likely to get paid a higher salary, which suits their stature and personality.

Hygiene and Grooming

It's important that men establish and maintain healthy hygiene habits for the good of their physical and mental health, their relationships, and their quality of life.

Head and Face

This is quite possibly the most integral part of your body that you can never ignore. Your face serves a great many purposes than just looking pretty: The way you look at someone, the way you smile and speak, the expressions of pleasure and charm that come across your face. And being the part of the body that is always in full view of everyone makes its grooming completely essential.

Daily habits such as brushing and flossing your teeth in the morning and at night create excellent oral hygiene. Following that, if you shave, then shave regularly or keep your facial hair well-groomed. Whether you go with a full-on beard or a distinguished mustache, seek out the style that complements you and highlights your masculine attraction, then commit to it and take excellent care of it. Use the best personal care products such as razors, trimmers, aftershave lotions, beard oils, combs, etc. to ensure that it all looks spick and span.

The same goes for your hairstyle, though that requires a bit more strategic selection. It all depends on the shape of your face. Study your face by pulling your hair back, and get a good look at how long and how wide your face is in a mirror. That means looking at how wide your forehead, cheekbones, jawline, and chin are, and if your face is long enough to be proportional. With oval face shapes, there are a lot of choices such as short, trimmed, buzzed, or even shoulder-length and modern cuts. Square-shaped faces have the advantage of a strong jawline, which provides opportunities to experiment with undercuts, longer lengths, and deeper side partitions. The key with square-shaped faces is having more volume and fullness in your hair. Round faces are somewhat of a challenge, as they leave no room to give an angular and distinct look. A hairstyle with longer fullness on the top and shorter sides will give your face a more angular and modern look (Vagus, 2019).

If you suffer from a genuine medical condition such as acne, then treat it with an appropriate face wash made for acne-prone skin. For spot treatment of pimples, use benzoyl peroxide cream sparingly when they pop up. But for any recurring or prolonged problems, do consult with your doctor. Remember, this could be a failing that you can improve by seeking out professional advice.

Depending on your facial features and shape, select a hairstyle that suits you and makes you feel at ease. Your hairstyle isn't just about creating attraction, but also should be selected on how comfortable you are with it. If it is too much of a hassle to maintain particularly in a public setting, then do away with it. That kind of discomfort becomes apparent to the people you meet with. Use hair care products such as shampoos, conditioners, and styling oils that are best suited to your hair. Commercially available products can cause lasting damage if used over time, so look for the ones that don't just present your hair in the best light, but also enrich it. A visit to a dermatologist can provide you with the right kind of products for your hair.

Body

It's not enough for your body to look good. The other senses have to come into play as well, so it's important that your body appears to be fit and alluring, both dressed and undressed. After all, that is one of the goals here, too.

Stay fresh by showering daily and frequently, depending on the weather and your activities. Next, use antiperspirant and/or deodorant, depending on your particular concern. While dressing, go easy on the cologne. Apply just a few dabs or sprays of cologne to areas like your neck or the insides of your wrists if you want to wear a fragrance. Wash your hands frequently or use an antibacterial hand sanitizer, as well as keeping your nails trimmed and tidy. You'll be using your hands quite a bit while dealing with both men and women, so make sure they feel nothing but pleasure when your hands come in contact with them.

For the rest of your body, be sure to focus on hygiene. Dispose of any clothes for washing once you're done with them, and be sure to change your underwear daily. Furthermore, consider a regular manscaping regimen to keep your body hair trimmed and neat. Trimmed body hair will make your physically fit body feel more tempting to touch once the clothes come off. Trimming your underarm hair with a pair of clippers does a lot for your hygiene as it reduces the amount of sweat you give off and thus minimizes body odor. Plus it helps you to smell wonderful with your preferred brand of antiperspirant.

As for your pubic hair, you may not want to shave it off entirely, and you don't even have to. However, keeping it trimmed and short actually makes you feel a lot more comfortable while wearing close-knit clothing and reduces the possibilities of annoyingly scratching yourself down there, even if you managed to do so without anyone noticing. Plus it makes you feel a lot more attractive and liberated, and works wonders for your partner once in bed. Lastly, if you have thick back hair, try getting it waxed regularly (Myers, 2015).

Clothing and Attire

Regardless of the occasion you need it for, your clothing and attire needs to be carefully selected to be of the highest standards of quality, fashion, and exquisiteness. It must form a signature style that defines you as a person, as well as your charisma and energy. People can tell a great deal about the kind of person you are and the tastes you have by your clothing alone, so it stands to reason that you'll have to be very mindful of what you wear and how you wear it.

Clothing Dos and Don'ts

No matter what you select for the desired occasion, taking care of your clothes stands high on your list. Clothes should be ironed, lint-rolled and clean at all times before you wear them to a social engagement. Match your colors appropriately and use proper contrasts of colors where necessary. As highlighted above, wear clothes that fit you well enough to show you in an appealing light. They should make your body look like they have a proper V shape from shoulders down. You can have your clothes tailored, if needed, in order to achieve the perfect fit. This also means avoiding clothes that are baggy, ill-fitting, drooping, or loose. They will show you in a more laid-back light and also make you appear to not care enough to respect yourself with decent clothes. Hint: betas.

Suits are the gold standard for exclusivity and exquisiteness, so these project you as the ideal alpha male. Have a selection of dark colored suits in different hues that don't just reflect your personality, but also suit your build and facial features. Your belt and shoes should also match in color, and your belt should look new and not worn out. Similarly, keep your shoes clean and shiny. Speaking of shoes, be sure to have a certain variety of them depending on the mood and the situation. Classic styles such as brogues, loafers, or a plain, dark, five-eyelet derby on a round toe are both stylish and appropriate for a wide variety of social situations.

Also have a collection of ties that complement your collection of shirts. Keep your underwear a simple affair, nothing too gaudy or embarrassing (Sims, 2020).

Dressing for the Occasion

Having an extensive wardrobe makes you well-organized and well-prepared for nearly every single social situation possible. You wouldn't want to be caught dead wearing something completely inappropriate to a certain event. Being dressed appropriately means you're dressed for success, and your own sense of style sets you apart from the crowd. Look into the kinds of attire worn in different events such as formal, casual, business casual, and black tie. Then begin amassing your own collection of suitable clothes.

While this is an investment in itself, don't be daunted by the monetary implications. You don't necessarily have to spend a fortune on nice clothes to form your own look, just have to spend enough to not look like you're buying budget wear or something that your mother picked out for you. Feeling the fabric in your hands and looking at the subtlety of the colors and appearance will help you decide just what you need in terms of quality, appeal, and price.

Accessorizing

Anything additional to your clothes acts as decorative items to make you feel more sophisticated. In this particular case, follow the doctrine of less is more. Items such as sunglasses, watches, leather bags, hats, leather wallets, etc. add unique and distinct touches to your outward appearance while also complementing your sense of style. Keep them simple and not too gaudy. With watches, go for classy timepieces for your nightlife while keeping smartwatches for your more active pursuits.

Fashion Rules to Abide by

While the above covers a holistic approach to your styling needs, keep a few useful reminders to perfect your outward appearance. Whenever on the go or standing, always button the top button of your coat or blazer, and never use the bottom one. As for your suits, dry clean them only twice a year while brushing away dirt after every wear. Furthermore, give them at least a day to air out to keep them fresh.

For denim, wash them every few months and wait at least six months before the first wash. Never put a shoulder strap with a tailored garment and, whenever the situation requires it, roll the sleeves of your shirt about two folds and no more.

For bespoke tailoring, ensure a good fit on the waist of your trousers. This is important to maintain a smart and clean silhouette. Similarly, make sure the shoulders of your blazers feel comfortable and fall in line flawlessly with your actual shoulders.

Always match your leathers, such as belts, shoes, wallets, key fobs, and even your phone case (Bryant, n.d.).

Being in Shape

The goal of being in shape for an alpha male doesn't necessarily mean being buff or chiseled out of marble. Popular media such as movies, TV shows and even comic books will project an ideal physique that influences us to appear a certain way. Nevertheless, it requires constant effort and discipline to achieve a physical appearance worthy of your stature as an alpha male. That is to say you don't have to look like Thor to attract beautiful women, but a close approximation increases your chances to be noticed immediately by the fairer sex. It is this kind of physical attraction that needs you to devote time and energy into your body, health, and state of mind.

Clean Up your Diet

In order to achieve the ideal body shape, it's necessary to eat right and avoid food that makes you look unattractive. Men are more muscular than women, which means they use up more calories a day than women. Depending on your body mass index, which is derived from your height and body mass as well as your level of activity, you will need anywhere from 2,200 to 2,800 calories a day. Therefore, look for foods with the right balance of calories, energy, and nutrients. Eating whole-grain foods such as bread, pasta, cereal, brown rice, oats, barley, etc. provides a great deal of energy and even reduces the risk of diseases, including prostate and colon cancers. Other grains such as beans, lentils, fruits and vegetables etc. have a high fiber content. This helps to control hunger and creates the illusion of fullness, so you don't eat or snack unnecessarily.

Seafood and plant-based foods such as beans, peas, and soy provide a healthy variety of protein to the body. Fat isn't something that you should be completely afraid of, but avoid saturated fat that does nothing but add unnecessary and unattractive layers to your body. Reduce saturated fat that is normally rich in high-fat meats and full-fat dairy products, not to mention oily and fried (fast) foods. A better alternative is using olive and canola oil, nuts, seeds, and avocados. These provide you with unsaturated and healthy fats that are actually more efficient and friendly when it comes to your cardiovascular system.

When we say reduce saturated fat, we don't mean remove it entirely. Saturated fat contains cholesterol which, while it makes you think about unhealthiness and disease, is actually a precursor to natural testosterone. Meanwhile, meat from fatty fish such as salmon contains polyunsaturated fat, which greatly regulates blood circulation and flow. Not only is it important for your health overall, but as an alpha male, it gets your libido going like anything.

Other habits such as skipping breakfast—or delaying it—can lead to an increase in the growth hormone and even losing a few pounds. Nevertheless, all of the above does not necessarily apply to everyone, particularly those with underlying medical conditions. It would be best to consult with a registered dietician or a nutritionist to find the healthy habits ideal for you.

Workout Regimen

While getting yourself a gym membership is great, you don't have to start off with one if you're beginning to get your body into shape. Keeping all the advice related to diet and foods in mind, you can easily begin a workout routine at home that will make you look, feel, and be healthier.

Whether you're looking to lose a few pounds or toning your physique, working out at home allows you to get into the right frame of mind and body to consider joining a gym full-time. Working out at home doesn't even need a great deal of equipment or even weights. Most, if not all, of the movements in weight training exercises can be performed by using your body's own weight for resistance, such as push-ups, sit-ups, and squats. Gradually, you can add adjustable dumbbells appropriate to your experience. A wide variety of apps are available that help you track your indoor exercise regimen while also suggesting newer workouts that you can perform easily at home (Bornstein, 2015).

Outdoor activities such as running, jogging, or cycling can also add endurance training to your workout routine and even improve your stamina, breathing, and cardiovascular circulation. They also help you to lose weight if you're looking to shed a few pounds and not be completely cooped up indoors by working out at home.

Once you find yourself with a better physical form and endurance than you had before, you can then get a lot more serious about your workout regimen. Enlist the services of a professional trainer or register at a gym that suits your needs. Increase the intensity of your workouts without straining your body too much too quickly. Sooner or later, you'll be able to deadlift from a deficit for maximum results.

And don't forget: Get plenty of rest. A good night's sleep for more than seven hours is ideal for most adults.

Projecting Confidence

Creating the ideal appearance by following the above guidelines for your attire, hygiene, grooming and physical health, you are able to project the right kind of confidence that is part and parcel of the alpha male. All of the above helps you to become naturally attractive physically and psychologically, and your behavior follows as you begin to carry yourself more distinctly than the rest. Your confidence makes you appear more self-assured and instantly attractive, which makes people want to be around you as much as possible. Oozing confidence as an alpha male increases the people in your orbit and provides you with even more opportunities to let them be in awe of you.

There might even be times when you're not feeling particularly confident, but all of the above elements and your habits and movements will readily compensate for any inner apprehensions you may have. The littlest of acts such as adjusting your posture a certain way can alter your mood significantly.

Confident Posture and Movement

Keep your posture straight and upright to look more confident and attentive. Slouching while standing is unappealing and also makes you look lazy. This also applies to when you sit down, so keep your spine straight while seated as well. Pulling your shoulders back and exposing your chest area gives an inviting and welcoming feeling, so don't slump either. To keep yourself more open, keep your legs and arms uncrossed.

Always show the people you're speaking to—especially women—that you're focused solely on them. Maintain eye contact and keep your chin up. Eyes forward and gaze aloft shows how much you value the person, and it also keeps your gaze from traveling downward to cause any obvious embarrassment.

Maintain a positive body language that shows steady and sure hand movements. Avoid fidgeting, as it can show any nervousness you're feeling on the inside. And while we're on that subject, touching your face, neck, or hair awkwardly are telltale signs of nervousness and make it appear as if you're trying to think of an appropriate response. Even if you are, it doesn't do well to make it more apparent. Also, don't forget to keep your hands visible, which means avoid putting them in your pockets. Your hands are extensions of your words as they provide the appropriate gestures to complement what you're saying. They can effectively project self-assuredness and expertise in what you're speaking about. As for your movements, keep them slow, even, and methodical. Being too fast, sudden, or haphazard with your movements will make you appear more anxious and unwelcoming.

Chapter 4

Drawing Them In

If you're under the impression that building yourself up with the right clothes, the right grooming, and the right physical frame should be more than enough to build connections with people—especially women—then you may want to get a reality check. Once you've accomplished getting the ideal alpha-male appearance and physique that is necessary to boost your confidence and catch the eye of the ones you wish to attract, the next stage begins. And this requires a lot more skill and persistence than you may have been using while working on your outward appearance to create an attraction. It requires having a charm and flair about you in the way you speak, the way you smile, and the way you act with women. How you look can certainly attract their attention, but to truly draw them in, you'll need to bring out your ultimate alpha-male personality.

The Art of the Approach

A true test for an alpha male to be in control of the environment is to use sharp observation skills before actually making a move. This takes place during the approach when an alpha enters the field where his intended goal is located. Despite a sea of beautiful women out there, the best ones to approach usually have to be in the ideal circumstances for you to use your skills to the fullest. And once you're able to see just the one you want to move on, your approach has to be both mysterious and alluring, and not at all unwanted.

Don't forget though that beautiful women do want to be approached. This is important as it lets them feel more beautiful and flattered if a handsome man such as yourself singles them out with your attention. Nevertheless, there may also be times when they are not ready or willing to be approached, so charging their way headfirst is definitely not the way to go.

Observe and Evaluate

Take a good look around her and carefully notice all the subtle signs before you actually make the approach. The environment around her can give you a hint as to who she is and what she's doing here. Does she have a smile on her face or is she more carefree as she hangs out with her friends? What is she wearing and how is she carrying herself? Is she herself dressed to impress or is this something new to her as well? Then look for some more obvious signs. Is there a wedding ring? It's not that hard to find out, or even notice if she's taken it off for the night if there's a bit of an impression around her finger. If her slurring speech is anything to go by, has she had a little too much to drink?

Plus it doesn't hurt to make a few other observations that may be probable. How comfortable is she around her friends? If she's at a venue where both genders are mingling, it's likely her tastes are more straight. Nevertheless, is she looking at one of her friends a bit more keenly than she should? How often is she touching her? Does it look casual enough, or is there something more?

And in case she's there all by herself, what do you think she's here for? Does she look open to anything, or is she a bit terrified inside? Does she look guarded or anxious? All of this must be observed in the few footsteps you take around her before turning your attention.

Be Felt and Not Seen

While you're making your observations, it is important that she doesn't actually notice you around her. Loitering is a big no, and you don't want to come across as a stalker. Use the people present to navigate carefully around her, and when the time is right, make your presence known. This should be done without really approaching her; simply give her an idea that she's being noticed. Let her see you in her peripheral vision and get her subconscious associated with your presence.

Once you've entered into her line of sight, move in for the briefest of moments and then move out again. Do all of this without actually looking at or speaking to her. Then, when she nudges her head up anxiously to see if you'll notice her or not, catch her eye and treat her with a smile. This shouldn't take longer than a few seconds, which means you mustn't keep eye contact with her for too long. Get a glimpse of her response and figure out what it is. Is she in your thrall? Is she just a tad disappointed that you've moved on? Is there something in her eye that shows her hope for more? The smaller the detail the better, as it shows how well you pay attention to the little things.

Make Your Move

Once you've tested the waters and determined whether an approach is worth the effort, it's time. Bring out your best smile, stay naturally positive, and approach her while she can see you, i.e. from her front or her side. Never approach from behind, and keep a considered distance from her so as to not intrude in her space. A yard or so apart should do nicely so that she doesn't find it uncomfortable. Keep your body relaxed while standing upright and confident.

Don't mess it up even before you start—and that means avoiding the cliches you've come to think actually work in breaking the ice with women. First and foremost: Never use pick up lines. This shows how little you understand the woman of today and lack awareness on what actually stimulates her. She'll automatically understand that you do not value or respect her at all, which is a huge alpha don't. Pick-up lines never work, and women instantly lose interest and walk away as soon as you utter one. If you are going to say something, make it something original, and make it count.

By the same token, don't offer to buy her a drink. You might think it's the gentlemanly thing to do, but why would you think she can't afford to pay for her own drinks? Also, what does it say about you as a person that you can buy her time for as little as a glass of alcohol? An offer to buy her a drink is an amateur ice-breaker as you do absolutely nothing substantial to introduce yourself. Rather, you automatically put yourself in a subordinate position which makes you desperate for her attention. Whereas the goal should be creating mutual interest in each other, offering to buy doesn't paint you as a self-respecting individual capable of carrying out a conversation, or as interesting in any way.

Most of the time, she'll be having a fun night out with a friend or a group, in which case be careful when you step in. If she's deep in conversation with a friend or listening to someone else tell a story, don't interrupt. Barging in and hijacking a conversation to gain attention is just plain rude. In fact, don't even single her out. Make it a point to address her friend or the group. Singling her out might make her feel insecure under your intentions, and it would no doubt lead her friends to feel protective of her. However, they may feel differently if you befriend every one of them and treat them as equals before gradually giving more and more of your attention to the one you are here for. And of course, it always helps if her friends see you in a positive light, which lets her know that they think you're alright. That is reassuring as well as polite on your part (Andrew Moore, n.d.).

The Conversation

Knowing what not to say and how to actually engage in getting her time, the next stage is to know exactly what to say that will make her interest in you deepen even further. The topics you touch upon will show her the kind of nature you have and the opinions you hold, which provide a direct window into your personality. It offers her a chance to evaluate you as well to determine whether or not you're compatible with each other, and if you are the sort of person she can see herself connecting with.

Start off with making casual observations about your surroundings, asking her what she thinks about the venue, and even solicit her feedback or opinion on a playful subject. Getting her to open up makes her feel that you want to hear more from her and value her opinions, and adding your own quips and responses to keep the conversation going shows the level of interest you have. Approaching her with questions also allows you to reveal as little of yourself as possible so as to keep an aura of mystery about you which keeps her guessing.

Speak Clearly

Once you've started your conversation, adjust your speech according to the environment you are in. You may want to speak a little louder than usual, particularly if the place is too crowded, and speak even louder if there's a lot of music and bustle making it hard to hear. In any circumstances, speak clearly and legibly without mumbling or eating your words. Keep a reasonable pace without going too fast so that she can keep up with you.

Respect her Time

While you've made headway in getting to know her a lot better, don't detract from why she came here in the first place. If her friends are with her then it may be a girls' night, in which case you don't want to be the odd one out. Letting her enjoy her time with her friends and withdrawing with a smile on your face lets her realize how much of a gentleman you are, and you may even tell her as much by saying you'd love to continue the conversation. Realizing how willing you are to let her have her fun as planned, she would want to extend you the same courtesy by exchanging phone numbers. This is indeed a success as you've got yourself the foundation of a sure connection. Both of you know there will be plenty of chances to talk later, which is actually a positive outcome.

Be Prepared for Rejection

Of course, there's an equal amount of chances that she'll say no at any stage of your interaction. It could be when you're making your move or during your conversation. There could be plenty of reasons for this, but it's best not to dwell on it. The moment she says no or gives no indication of carrying on, be a good sport about it and flatter her with a smile. A simple "Well, it was worth a shot. Enjoy your evening!" goes a long way to leave a positive opinion of both the interaction and you. After all, there's no need for the evening to end on a sour note, and that's not how you want to feel if you wish to make a move on your next prospect (*How to Ask for Her Number (and Actually Get It)*, n.d.).

Charisma

Ever wonder why alpha males have women swooning over them and they're seen with someone new every day? It might be because of the way they look or flaunt themselves, but a much more natural way is having charisma. It is the quality of being able to attract, charm, and influence those around you, a mixture of both affability and influence. Having charisma is what allows you to command a room, draw others toward you, and convince people of your ideas. In short, they'll be hanging on to your every word because of the charisma you exude.

Of course, being charismatic is possible with effort and practice. The key to developing charisma in yourself is to focus on certain traits you can practice every day and then apply to your own behavior that will make you seem more magnetic, trustworthy, and influential. Different aspects of charisma work their way to create a sort of magic within you that you can use to draw people in and become someone they can hardly ever avoid.

Presence

You might think that charisma is all about you, but the paradoxical secret behind it is quite the reverse. Having charisma isn't just about blowing your own trumpet and branding yourself as God's gift to humanity. It is about making others feel valued in your own presence. The more comfortable and respected they feel around you, the more their loyalty to you increases. They will see you as someone interactive, pleasant, and cheerful enough to make them feel good about themselves, and to not have to be on their guard when they're around you. To them, there's nothing you can say or do that will make them want to leave your orbit, and that all begins with how you treat them when they're with you. Remember, less about you and more about them. Don't ever put others down, no matter what (McKay, 2013).

Power

The way you look and the manner you move or do things creates an aura of perfection about you. People will want to be seen next to you for the power you have over yourself and your environment, with your body language and appearance making you stand out among the crowd and creating a bubble of safety and security with your confident stride. Your subtle gestures and expressions also convey that you're paying them the attention they want. A smile, a nod, or even a frown can let them know you've been listening to what they've been saying. Affirming them or even confirming your understanding with some good questions can also show how well you understand their meaning. Also, don't glare or stare at them as they might feel insecure. Simply keep your eyes ever so lightly on theirs and let your smiles and nods do the rest. Most importantly, don't glance over their shoulders, especially if you spot a more interesting target across the room. And that goes double for getting distracted by your phone.

Warmth

Once your presence as a cheerful and pleasant person lets them feel comfortable, developing genuine warmth with them happens relatively easily. It's all about being approachable, caring, and empathetic to them. Genuine warmth makes you feel their pain and apprehensions as if they were happening with you, and makes you invested in their well being. You want them to feel better. You need them to feel good about themselves by your words and actions. Above all else, you want them to feel better thanks to you. Not that it means you owe them anything, but it creates a warm feeling inside you of a job well done. Nevertheless, don't be fake when trying to empathize. Start with a simple, low-key, and curious approach to your interactions with others. They may gradually become comfortable enough to open up to you, so know the best version of yourself. Charisma is all about consistently revealing who you are at your own pace—sometimes confidently, sometimes quietly.

Charm

Charm is simply the art of letting someone know that you feel good about them, without asking anything from them in return. That in effect makes them feel good about you, too, and a mutual connection is formed. Being charming is all about creating feelings of attraction for yourself inside of a woman, as well as being the kind of person who's pleasant to be around, talk to, and interact with.

There is no way to actually make yourself or force yourself to be charming. It has to be sincere and come from a place of genuine care. It is most powerful when you believe what you're saying as the more you believe it, the realer it becomes.

Once you understand what people find charming and practice it over and over again to the point of perfection, it will become part of your personality and second nature, which makes you more endearing to others.

A Simple Equation

Yes, using an equation for attraction might seem unusual, but being charming with women is actually that simple. The equation is this:

Make her feel attracted to you + Treat her nicely = Charming

That's right, be your genuine alpha self and show her what a caring and compassionate person you are. And who better to be caring and compassionate to than her? To be charming, think less about appearing to be impressive to her, and more about being warm and friendly using your charisma. You should also be concerned about whether the other person feels like they're performing well, too (Bacon, n.d.-a).

Practicing Charm

There's no better time to practice your charm than being in the moment itself, so the trick is to be totally captivated by her as a person, as well as every word she says to you. That means giving her your undivided attention and never interrupting or stopping the flow of her conversation. It shows how much you value her as a person and her ideas. So talk less, listen more. Instead of talking about yourself and trying to impress her, be impressed by her. You may even recall a certain memory that completely relates to what she's telling you about, and you might even want to tell her about it. Don't. Don't make it about you. Talk and listen as if you find her to be the most fascinating person you've ever met.

It isn't even that hard to do. Hang on her every word, but do ask questions sometimes and listen closely to the answers. It shows how interested and curious you are about her as a person. See how long you can encourage her to speak without interrupting or talking about yourself. The more impressed you are by her, her ideas and opinions, her character and personality, the more impressed she will be with you.

The Art of Body Language

Body language accounts for about 55% of what you convey when you speak. The way you move your hands, the ease with which you sit in your seat without showing any discomfort, as if the thought of your message were making you cringe (Barker, 2012).

Several studies show that women can read body language two to three times better than men. Your body language should let women feel that you are welcoming and open to them. Adopt an open position by keeping your arms visible, not folded as it shows reservedness. Stand with feet shoulder width apart, arms at belt level, and head held high. The more poised, open, and self-assured you appear, the more comfortable others will feel approaching you.

Keeping eye contact lets you direct your positive energy toward them, making it more likely that they will be drawn to you. Locking eyes with someone can be tricky for both of you, so if you feel a bit awkward staring into someone else's eyes, try this little trick: Draw an imaginary inverted triangle on the other person's face around their eyes and mouth. During the conversation, change your gaze every five to ten seconds from one point on the triangle to another. This will make you look interested and engrossed in the conversation.

Smiles go hand in hand, so always smile with a genuine, heartfelt, smile. The more you smile, the more positive feelings you invoke in yourself and the people around you.

When you feel the tension rising, be extra mindful of your body language and keep it positive. Lean forward during conversation, as opposed to leaning back to create a distance. That's exactly what leaning back does: Creates distance between you two. But be mindful not to slouch while leaning forward, either. It takes practice to find your sweet spot, and it becomes one of your best assets when you do.

Keep a firm handshake under all circumstances. A weak handshake is a sign of a lack of confidence, and people will pick up on it. Mirror their actions, but don't imitate.

Reading Body Language

Remember that all your actions are being observed closely, and vice versa. While you have to keep your body language as welcoming and accommodating as you possibly can, there might be something that could put them off which they won't make obvious verbally, but their actions or gestures could tell you all you need to know. Understand the context in which you notice certain movements and figure out if someone should be acting the way they are in this particular situation. It may not even be just one kind of action, as it may have a few other tics that form a whole cluster of actions. What are these behaviors associated with? Discomfort? Apprehension? Fear?

Once you get those out of the way, get a baseline for how they normally act. Look for telltale signs of what makes them happy, excited, and even sad. This way, you know how to act or react accordingly. The same applies with how you behave yourself as well. Do away with the quirks and tics that can signal your own discomfort and create your own baseline full of confidence, charm, and charisma.

Be aware of your biases, however. Don't presume or assume anything even before they've started to speak. As an alpha male, your goal is to create a lasting connection and she'll be more drawn toward you if you take the time to understand her vulnerabilities. This is also going to be new for her as well; never forget that.

Will She or Won't She?

Depending on how well your interaction is going with her, body language can tell you whether or not she's ready to explore further. If she starts moving toward you and decreasing the space between you, it's a clear tell that she's beginning to enjoy your company and your presence. It's even better if she's leaning toward you or has her feet pointing toward you. The distance continues to diminish and her yearning for you begins increasing, which is why she'll have her legs uncrossed and comfortable. Keeping her arms open and visible along with her palms up, not to mention playfully fondling her jewelry or hair shows how much fun she's having with the interaction. Above all else, her smiling, making extended eye contact, and especially looking down shyly as she pushes strands of her hair behind her ear just about seals the deal.

There are other positive indicators which may not seem like a good omen at first. For instance, she may even lose her bearings if she finds your level of attraction a lot more intense than either of you thought. This can turn her confident and assertive self into someone who's tongue-tied and even gaga at you. This may seem cute at first but may lose its charm if you're looking to move past your initial stages of conversation. But be ready to give her a chance to get her bearings and help her come out of her reverie. If she's at a loss for words, you can even carry the conversation for a bit and be playful about the whole thing. Give her some room to breathe so that she can overcome her nervousness. Keep in mind that if she's fumbling or at a loss for words, it's very likely because she wants to make the best impression on you as well.

Conversely, if she starts moving away, turning her eyes away from you, scratching around her eyes or nose, rubbing the back of her neck, or nodding a lot more, then you have a problem. The nodding should make it obvious: You're talking way too much. Not only that, you're most definitely mansplaining, which is exactly why she's frowning and grimacing. Keeping her eyes away from you should sound alarm bells in your head, and you can forget about any welcoming if she's got her legs crossed and stiff, palms down, and hands closed.

While we're on the subject, your own disinterest can become obvious to her as well. It may be involuntary, but your microexpressions can also trigger something in her that will ultimately turn you off. It may happen for even the briefest of moments, but if she picks up on it, it can change her entire outlook of the whole experience. They reveal some truths you may have been trying your best to hide, but failed to do so in a split second. Nevertheless, try your best to remain actively engaged in the conversation and let her feel with your body language that you are just as invested in it as she is (Nicholson, 2011).

Chapter 5

Keeping Them Interested

You've caught her eye and gained her attention. You've managed to successfully make her friends adore you. You've made a place for yourself in her mind and her body begins to get comfortable around you with your casual wit, your magnetic charm, and your magical charisma. And it looks like you've done really well for starters. Now you've got to keep her engaged and invested in you to make her realize that you're all this and so much more. That's why first impressions are just that: The first. It's important to engage and build rapport from there on, which means keeping your alpha game on when it comes to flirting.

Flirting 101

Flirting is meant to be a light, fun interaction with a breezy sexual vibe and sweet validation. Ultimately, the goal is to get her to smile and keep smiling. Believe it or not, most men have absolutely no clue on how to flirt with women at all. Instead, they attempt whatever comes to them with the least amount of observation and hope for the best to just happen. You can take a good guess on how that ends up: Awkward and full of embarrassment, especially if other people—read: women—watch you crash and burn.

This is where your alpha-male personality traits come into play and your skills at communication make your case for you. Be a great conversationalist by leading the discussion in the direction you wish to, but keep it fun and interesting for both of you. You'll see from her welcoming body language just how receptive she is to your flirtations, so make her comfortable enough to open up and get her talking about the things she loves. Think of something witty and funny to say that will complement what she has to say and make her laugh instantly. Avoid sexual jokes and toilet humor at all costs, and don't make jokes at your own expense. She should be laughing with you and not at you.

Don't Fall for Clichés

Obviously you're not pursuing a liaison unless she's attractive physically, so it stands to reason that a lot of other men have tried their luck in charming her. She knows just how beautiful she is and what features of her attract men toward her like moths to a flame, so take a guess as to how many pick-up lines and material she's heard and been bored by. While other men make the mistake of using boring and passé material that has been done to death, you need to avoid it like the plague. So none of the angels falling from heaven or stealing your heart routines, unless you want to be laughed out of the club.

Be original and natural with the way you approach her. Use your own sense of confidence and self-assuredness. Your mastery of style and posture, as well as your charm, need to be emanated in the way you talk to her. The words you use have to be classy, original, and full of social grace that won't make her roll her eyes or turn her smile into an uncomfortable one.

Keep It Breezy

Once the conversation enters the stage where she expects you to be cheerful and talkative, don't disappoint her. You've been complimenting her opinions thus far, but now it's time to be more humorous and playful. Banter helps a great deal as you find several similar interests, and you can keep it lively and positive with some clean and funny jokes and playful teasing. Knowing the right thing to say is going to be important, as it will the conversation flowing at a natural pace. Never grunt or make uncomfortable sounds while you listen to her, or she'll perceive it as a lack of interest. Don't forget to show positive body language as well to show that you're interested. Plus it leads to the next and most challenging part: touch (*7 Tips on Flirting With Women*, n.d.).

As a rule, hold off on complimenting her until later. You don't want to hand her a birthday present and tell her explicitly what it is before she even unwraps it, do you? And anyway, you're here and talking to her, which is more than enough for her to realize just how worthy she is of your praise. All the mystery and excitement is taken out of the encounter, so leave that for when the time is right. That should let you two engage with each other over a wide variety of topics, especially if it's talk that makes her feel good about herself without actually complimenting her. Looking at her with desire in your eyes, holding her gaze as you converse, makes her feel like the most wanted woman in the world, which brings her yearning to be complimented to a fever pitch. This is what you should play around with as it offers you a great opportunity to be your confident and sexy self. She'll want you soon enough, but having a little fun along the way is actually more endearing.

Playful Use of Double Entendres

You might be thinking "wait, this sounds like juvenile behavior," but it doesn't have to be. Double entendres, if timed and done right, can prove to be both fun and playful without sounding too coarse or vulgar. It adds small pricks—pun not intended—of the sexual into a conversation without being the actual goal. Instead, it can be entertaining and ideal to have a good laugh about. Plus, they don't even have to be sexual in their double meanings to be funny (*How To (Properly) Flirt With A Woman (Updated 2020)*, 2017).

Even unintentional double entendres can elicit a laugh, and it's even more endearing if she gets the joke and you don't. Letting her be the one creating the laughter and entertainment makes the conversation a lot more light-hearted and you can nudge it toward being interpreted as sexual, without making it look deliberate.

Treating Her Right

Always be gentle, respectful, and kind. That's the way to go to create the best impression of yourself in her mind. Nevertheless, don't be too coy and instead be straight about who you are, what you want, and what your interests are. Keeping your expectations managed as well as hers will make sure that you're both in agreement about the outcome of your rendezvous and not under any assumptions that either of you aren't ready for yet.

Right off the bat when you come to pick her up from her place, be a gentleman. Open the car door for her and hold her hand as she steps inside. The same goes for when you arrive at the restaurant or event, unless the valet is at hand. Remember that you consider her to be special, so offer your hand or elbow as you lead her inside. You won't even need to pull a chair out for her if she has her hand in yours.

The goal of a date is to show her a good time and how considerate you are of her feelings and emotions. Thus, plan an itinerary that you know she'll enjoy. Candlelight dinners, long walks along the promenade, taking in a show of her liking—basically make it an evening she won't soon forget.

The Little Things

Don't forget to pick up the check on your date, always and with no exceptions. You're the alpha male, and it's part of being a gentleman to treat her to the perfect night and make sure her experience is both seamless and enjoyable. The only time you can and should make an exception to this if she absolutely demands to get it herself. It is better to let her pick up some or all of it than to enter a debate—or even worse, fight about it. Of course you can insist for a bit until you get the feeling that she isn't about to budge, in which case be graceful about it and show her you care for her gesture.

Little gestures go a long way to add more value to your experience and improve her opinion of you. Clasp her hand as you go out on walks, even if you're walking to your car. Keep looking at her as much as possible and notice her body language. If you feel that she's a bit cold and shivering, offer her your jacket and put it on her slowly and carefully to show how caring you are of her needs.

Respect Her as a Person

Yes, she's attractive, and yes the two of you look amazing together with her incredible beauty and you with your alpha charm. But that doesn't mean that's all there is to either of you. Remember that she is a person with her own self-respect and ambitions, and always has been even before you came into her life. While she's here and giving you her time, you would do well to remember that this is because she has given you a privilege which you shouldn't idly squander. Treat her with the respect she deserves and look beyond her good looks. Surely she's also thinking quite highly of you for being a gentleman through and through, so it doesn't do well to ruin that impression.

Let her Take Control, Too

By now, your flirting game with her is getting quite exciting, but don't forget to let her have some fun, too. Your playful banter has gotten her all excited, which means she's ready to be playful with you. It's essential that she not be restrained from showing you her affections, as not only does it offer you an immediate reward, but she also gets to show you how she feels about you. Plus as an alpha male, you set yourself apart by being pampered by her for a change, which isn't something she might expect from other men.

Not only that, getting her to flirt with you makes her feel how much in control she is of the evening and increases her confidence greatly. It also makes her feel sexy and increases the level of attraction between you two. While you can make her feel desirable with the way you flirt with her, your responses and reactions to how she does the same with you makes her feel like quite the charmer in her own right. Plus it shows her level of interest toward how she wants things to go soon. While flirting both ways may provide some entertainment for both of you in the present setting, it may even serve as a prelude for other things yet to come, such as going for a walk in the promenade after dinner, being invited for coffee at her place, and of course, the opportunity for getting intimate.

The Art of Conversation

Right off the first meeting to subsequent dates or night outs, conversations can either make or break your connection with her. Good conversations give you the opportunity to showcase your intelligence, sense of humor, and even your *sexy* voice. According to singles, those are the top three things that have made a date appear more attractive to them.

Even so, there is tons of literature and research out there which highlight just how important great conversational abilities are for the ultimate dating experience. Janz, Pepping, and Halford (2015) found that heterosexual women thought men appeared more attractive when they were actively involved in the conversation rather than acting aloof. There's more: A newly released survey conducted by Plenty of Fish found that nine out of 10 singles say great conversation is the number one sign of a successful date. So it's not just a question of being able to hold a great conversation with her, but to be able to talk over a wide variety of topics that she'll find interesting as well as entertaining.

The secret behind great conversations isn't really all that secret. It just requires you to be natural and not to think of this as something that has to be too grand. As with all relationships and connections, commonalities are what bind two people together. Whether it's hobbies or interests or even the same food you two may have an affinity for, small talk can get you two to find out exactly what you have in common. The goal of small talk is to find points of similarity. This is important as having similarities is extraordinarily powerful when it comes to bonding. Even if there aren't any right off the bat, you can always be interested in knowing more about what she finds most interesting. She'll find that more important and caring instead of driving the conversation away from her areas of interest.

Making Great Conversation

The real benefit of small talk is that you're able to show genuine interest in wanting to know her well. It helps you to channel your curiosity and show true interest in her as a person, which she will find appealing. Remember, getting her to talk and opening up is essential for an alpha male to show how much you respect her, and thus you'll stir up some meaningful topics and questions to accomplish just that. Ask questions that are purposeful and open-ended, as you'll not only get yes or no answers, but also details on the hows and the whys behind them. Be open about how curious you are regarding certain topics, but try to keep it light, respectful, and open. Add juicy tidbits in your responses and embellish them with interesting and intriguing bits of information. For instance, if you're commenting on your last visit to a restaurant, sprinkle some additional information of how the atmosphere and ambiance was that time and make comparisons with how it usually is. Tidbits of information like this will allow her to strike something in her mind and add more to the conversation, even continue it along with you perhaps in a similar or tangential vein.

If at times it feels certain topics might be troubling for her to discuss—perhaps due to a negative experience—don't push on further but instead focus on the positives. Always look for ways to make her look and feel good. This way, you'll help her to overcome the negativity she may have and build her up to be much better than before after having gone through it. Treating her well and building up her confidence and self-image are great moves that will help everyone in the long run. Don't forget to encourage her and provide positive feedback. Drop compliments where appropriate, and recognize her talents when you see them. It all connects back to your charm and charisma.

Sometimes, without even intending it, the conversation may meander its way toward something a lot more sensitive such as religion, politics, etc. Remember, never judge or argue, and keep an open mind. It's really important not to awkwardly stop the conversation if the subject is a tad too sensitive. In fact, showing that you don't mind a light discussion over it is a sign that you don't mind discussing ideas that you may not be necessarily comfortable with. Besides, you can always agree to disagree if there are any clashes in ideas.

Tone of Voice

Ever heard of the 7-38-55 rule? It's a theory developed by Albert Mehrabian in 1971 when he was a psychology professor at the University of California. As a rule, it effectively lays out the communication of emotions in all sorts of high-stakes negotiations, and it doesn't get more high-stakes than conversing with your intended date. But what is this rule? Simply put, your body language accounts for about 55% of your communication, followed by the tone of your voice which accounts for about 33%. Only 7% is actually accounted for by the words you use (Mehrabian & Blum, 1997).

As we've seen how important body language is to your charm and personality, the tone of voice is not to be underestimated. The way you say something—regardless of what the words are—really, really matters, especially in the sphere of intimate relationships. You can effectively get your message across if you gain expertise in the different tones you use to deliver it. An assertive tone can actually sound more forceful and pressuring, which can only damage things. Instead, use a more accommodating tone which makes her feel at ease with you and shows how caring and welcoming you are to her thoughts and ideas.

Also keep track of the pitch used by both you and her. Experience suggests that women spoke in a higher-pitched and less monotone voice on speed dates with men they chose as potential mates. However, if they sensed that a man was in strong demand, the high pitch immediately switched to significantly deeper pitches.

The trade-off implied by this dichotomy suggests that women may raise their voice pitch to signal youth and femininity, but lower their pitch in contexts where they wish especially to indicate sexual interest to a listener.

Similarly, men with low-pitched voices tend to have higher success in a range of social contexts, from mating to socio-economic and even political.

Keep Listening

Do not make it appear as if you weren't paying attention. Getting zoned out and disinterested just because she's going on about something you're not invested in can show clearly in your body language and tone of voice. If she has to ask whether you're listening to her or not, it ultimately means that you've dropped the ball here. Worse still, answering her that you are can make things head for disaster. Sprinkling her conversation with odd tidbits of information and even posing some questions to a few points will let her know that you are indeed all ears. Even sharing something similar in terms of how it happened but different in context can create a great deal of understanding between you two. For instance, her opinions and experiences about something out of popular culture may actually ring a bell in your knowledge about Roman mythology or ancient history. If you're able to make a connection and let her know of it, she's bound to have a eureka moment, and you'll notice from her excitement how glad she is that you *get* it.

Touch

By now you've gotten a handle of how welcoming she is with her body language, so the next logical stage once you get close enough is the touch. You'll know from how close her hands or feet are to you that she wouldn't mind you making a stray touch of her fingers or her arms. Even your knee brushing against her thigh would be most welcome.

Touch is an essential way to communicate and influence without words. When done in the right way, artful and carefully considered touch can make someone feel more attracted to you. It can also increase physical intimacy, which makes passionate kissing—and sexual activity—more likely. A clear indicator would be her making a move, which opens up all sorts of possibilities. Regardless, touch her gently without making it too obvious. Make it look like it's the most natural thing to you and something you do with comfort and ease.

Building Intimacy

To build passion and *chemistry*, it is important to increase the intimacy of touch over time (in just the right way). The first stage is social touching, i.e. starting with just the hands or shoulders with gentle and brief strokes to get her attention, or to handle interesting objects she may have. Keep it light, playful, and fun. Slowly move on to friendly touching once she becomes more comfortable with how you feel. Holding her hand for a moment or two will be a pleasure, as will giving her a hug or touching her shoulders. And once you're sitting next to each other, touching her legs is the next logical step toward introducing the intimate touch.

After getting comfortable, work on cuddling her closer to you in order to build more passion. Slowly put your arm around her and brush her hair away from her face affectionately. Hold her in your embrace closer and for longer periods of time. Then, when the moment is right, bring your lips to hers. And kiss.

The Sexual Touch

Sexual energy is not the same as sensual energy—let's be clear on that. While your buildup until now has developed the kind of intimacy you feel should be enough, it may vary from person to person and how they're feeling at the moment. Therefore, it's important to understand just how much you've been pleasing her sensually with the intimate setting.

Sensual energy uses all the senses of the human body to create a shared experience of pleasure that soothes us both physically and mentally. It's different from sexual as it may be the need of the moment where sexual activity may not be welcome just yet. Activities such as cuddling, feeling each other up, caressing, and of course kissing create a fully sensual experience that we can see, hear, smell, and touch, and allow us to remain in the moment of the experience.

On the other hand, sexual energy is not only more intimate, but also more intense. It has a singular goal of fulfillment which requires us to move from one point to another. Once the end goal of sex is accomplished, the moment feels more rushed and unfulfilling than it was before. Because we move on to sex a lot quicker than it is necessary, we put our sensual fulfillment on the backburner and miss out on sensually connecting with our partners on a more emotional level.

Graduating from an intimate and loving touch to a more sexually arousing one requires a bit more time and privacy, not to mention an emotional and sensual connection. However, if you've been touching her more gently and with greater consideration for slowly arousing her to a point where she feels deeply connected to you sensually, you can progress toward sex with comfort and ease.

Simply follow the steps above, then increase the passion of your kissing. Use tongue. Kiss and caress more vulnerable parts—including the neck and chest. Move your hands over the lower back, rear, thighs, etc. Then take it from there into foreplay and sex.

Other Kinds of Touch

Even in a situation that doesn't call for too much intimacy, touch is akin to an expansive science that requires mastery and practice to improve all sorts of relationships. Be it in a professional setting that requires you to be more interactive and proactive with your immediate colleagues, or with your close friends and relatives in a social setting, the power of touch should never be underestimated. It becomes a natural outlet for you to exude warmth, care, love, and affection, as well as sincerity, humility, and trust.

According to Richard Heslin, touch can be classified into five distinct categories that serve to create lasting bonds (Nicholson, 2012). The first is the functional or professional touch, which can be handshakes or even pats on the back. These are primarily used with immediate work colleagues including your managers and team members, as well as those who report to you. Next is the social or polite touch, which involves careful pats on the arm or shoulder, and can be done with social acquaintances. Taking it a step further from your social setting, your close friends and people you care for the most come next and deserve a lot more affection. This brings us to the friendship or warmth touch, and as it says, it allows you to radiate more friendliness and warmth by hugging and hand-holding.

The last two categories of touch, and the most intimate ones, are naturally reserved for the most important person in your lives. Whether it's to show love and intimacy with the woman of your dreams, or something far more sexual and arousing, the progression of touch can move from kissing, cuddling, and nuzzling to intimate encounters such as foreplay and sex, by caressing and using your tongue around the erogenous zones. And of course, the sex itself.

In any event, touch adds on to your relationship experiences as much as verbal and non-verbal communication does, if not more. As a romantic relationship begins and progresses, so too does the level and intensity of touch in your lives. Keep in mind that your current romantic liaison may have naturally started from a social setting and even progressed to friendship and affection before growing into an intimate relationship. Along with this progression, the touch starts from the parts of the body that aren't necessarily sexual and intimate, such as the hands, arms, shoulders, and even the upper back. If you follow this sequence with your intended partner, she can gain an understanding of how you feel and the warmth you give off, which creates even more of an attraction toward you. Ultimately, it allows you to move on to areas of the body that are more intimate, such as the lower back, neck, face, breasts, thighs, and eventually, under the lingerie.

Chapter 6

Getting It On

Things are heating up, and if you've played your cards right, it's about time the clothes come off. But even in the heat of the moment, an alpha male still has to maintain respect for a woman's boundaries and be sensitive to her signals. There could be any number of reasons why she may not want to have sex at the moment, aside from the obvious reasons, and though it's not an outcome you want, it's one you should be ready for. Getting physical should never be an obligation for the good time you showed her. If you've managed your expectations properly, you should remember that you're not owed any sex for creating a fun night for her and being the gentleman that you are. In fact, it's the hallmark of a true gentleman to be ready for rejection.

Still, let's stay positive for now and hope for the best. At best, you're looking forward to a night of passion and ecstasy. So let's keep that goal as a primary until the worst-case scenario happens.

Invitation for Sex

First things first: Her sexual rejection usually isn't about you. It could be her mood, her self-esteem in front of you, not being at the perfect stage of arousal, or something that's occupying her mind. In any case, it doesn't have to be because of you and it definitely isn't something you should aim to change. If she isn't in the mood, then the best course of action is to respect her wishes. Knowing that she may have all sorts of things on her mind, simply state that you understand and don't press for an answer. Be a bit playful about it, but don't make it obvious that you're hurt. Remember your alpha-ness and avoid whining about it. That's just a precursor to becoming an asshole, and you've worked far too hard for that.

On a positive note, the fact that you understand shows the level of maturity you possess, which is a winner in her eyes. Perhaps she's testing you or not, but being an alpha male, your behavior bumps your impression in her eyes once more. And maybe not this time, but the next time will be different.

The Come-On

It's time to bring your A-game to the table. Once she's shown no sign of refraining from getting it on, you'll have to make your come-on right at the moment. The best approach is always one that's more personalized to her attributes. The way you touch her sensually on the part you find most attractive—non-sexually at the moment—and the way she responds to your touch shows that she loves it when you pick that single, solitary spot to be just for the two of you. Sharing a couch and rolling your fingertips either clockwise or counter-clockwise around her knee can send her waves upon waves of pleasure, making her relinquish her defenses and want you even more. All because you send direct signals of how much you want her.

Another important aspect is making your intentions clear, and by this we mean clearer than crystal. Regardless of what it is you want to do, be it touching her body all night for the sheer pleasure of it or going down on her, you say it to her without beating around the bush—no pun intended. It can even be something less than glamorous, say a quickie in the bathroom, but it's always best to communicate this in any case. You can even think up an exotic scenario involving a specific kind of sexual encounter, which clears her mind on what you're expecting. Whisper what it is you want to do with her in a slow and intriguing voice. Make it a question of desire as you continue to touch her and simply mention to them that you'd like to try something such as a nude massage, etc. It creates a vivid picture for her to both understand and be inspired by. Best-case scenario: It works and you get exactly what you desire.

If your potential mate is someone you've just been *seeing* for a while but haven't had sex with yet, don't presume that she would like to have sex with you. Sure, you've been dating for a while and even gotten close enough for kissing, but that doesn't mean much, especially if she hasn't made it obvious until now. Be cool and have a brief chat about whether or not she's interested. You can let her know what your intentions are and that you find her attractive. If she shies away from talking about it, you may even ask about if there are any STI problems. You're both mature adults and shouldn't find this discussion to be too difficult, but in the case she does, be respectful and empathetic. Let her know it's okay to talk about this, or if she has any other aversions to doing the deed. The key is to make her feel at ease.

Before The Foreplay

Don't just limit yourself to the date and the foreplay itself. Let her know from way earlier that you're looking forward to meeting *all* of her. Start working on it from the beginning of the day by sending her text messages telling her how much you want her. Sexting may be frowned upon generally and may even appear to be gross on the face of it, but there is no reason why it shouldn't be a fun exercise that increases your interaction as well as builds her enthusiasm for when the time comes. Go with something flirty in the beginning and see what her response is like. Once you see her responses matching yours and even creating a stir, keep the conversation going throughout the day. Tell her about some of the scenarios you'd like to think about involving her, and make them as alluring and exciting as possible. Double entendres can be used once again, albeit more deliberately than ever before. Again, be prepared to be shut down here if she doesn't find this all too flattering, so don't press her too much and don't fret about it at all.

Casual Encounters

If it's a case of a casual hookup, though, you know exactly what both of you are expecting from the get-go. Still, that isn't any reason why it shouldn't be fun. Start with some genuine small talk to get to know a bit about one another. It makes things a lot less complicated and creates a bit of comfort before getting to bed. Small talk can clear up just how enthusiastic you are about the hookup and you'll be 100% sure that you actually want to have sex with her.

Be careful with casual encounters who are already in a relationship. It never hurts to find out in small talk if they are already in one, though they may not admit it right away. Ask about how come they're still single and the answers may come out. It's helpful to know if they are in any sort of relationship agreement, especially one that requires them to be monogamous. While open relationships are usually problem-free, it's the discreet ones that you should be wary of (Litner, 2020).

Consent

While an alpha male is assertive and may appear to be a "don't take no for an answer" kind of animal, being respectful of one's boundaries is essential to them. Especially in matters of sex, they value sexual consent a great deal for a wide variety of reasons. The most obvious is that given consent means free, full, and active agreement to engage in sexual activity. Consent should always be clear, knowing, and voluntary as it's essential for taking things to the next stage.

Never assume that consent is forever. It may have been given once for a moment, but that doesn't mean that it applies for all other times. If she's consented to one sexual encounter, don't take it as a given. She may change her mind at any stage, even while you're having sex. You may think she's joking around, but her body language and protests will be more than obvious. Not only does consent apply to the different times you may engage in sexual activity, but also to the different sexual acts. She may even deny you consent when you're taking the clothes off her body, or may be more than happy to have you go down on her but not return the favor when you want her to. Therefore, the responsibility of an alpha male is to renew and reconfirm with her repeatedly and continuously, and at different times and stages of the sexual encounters (*Disrespect NoBody | Consent | Recognising Consent*, n.d.).

Look for the Signs

While she may not say no outright, it may be what she's thinking or feeling and may express it in different ways. If her face contorts or shows discomfort, or her body tenses up, or she attempts to block you from going any further, or she pushes you away from even hugging her, and especially if she sounds like she's in pain, these are clear indicators that she's become an unwilling participant. Body language and non-verbal indicators are a lot more obvious than verbal ones, largely because she may not want to refuse you or risk upsetting you (Weiss, 2019).

But it does take a psychological as well as physical toll on her even as you push on further. Her non-consent may be due to multiple reasons you're not even aware of or she hasn't been able to tell you about. It may be due to fear for her physical safety in your hands or the social stigma associated with her family or society about having sex, especially out of wedlock. It could be due to shame she feels that she may not be as good in bed as you expect her to be, or even feel a lack of sexual desire. Sometimes she may be uncertain about having sex in the first place, which may or may not be because of you. Nevertheless, she may not have fully committed to the idea and is trying to figure out the best way to say no. And most importantly, she may be reliving a past trauma that has been triggered through the sexual acts.

Be Empathetic

Even though she may not be ready to give you a verbal refusal, it is your responsibility to ensure that she isn't feeling pressured into doing something. This would imply non-consent and that can lead you to extremely murky territory, both emotionally and even legally. Put yourself in her shoes and be empathetic to her desires, or lack thereof at the moment, and understand what she does or doesn't want. A direct yes or no question is the best approach and is far better than waiting for a sign from her. Nevertheless, do look out for the signs. Whenever in doubt, don't be afraid to stop and ask her outright, as it's the simplest way to find out if she consents or not. "Is this okay?" "Do you want this?" "Would you rather do something else?" "We can stop if you want to." While a direct answer should settle things easily, consider it a no if she gives no clear response or indication. She may be processing things and working out how you might react if she denies you, so it's better to be the bigger person and take this as a no.

Being empathetic to her needs is what sets you apart, as we've seen all through the previous chapters. Having a clear understanding between each other lets her know that you're willing to always take her consent into consideration and be a responsible and mature adult about it. It is a hallmark of your maturity as an alpha male that you understand that not wanting to have sex is a natural tendency not just in women, but in men as well. Furthermore, you're not owed sex just because it's the next stage in your relationship. If either of you doesn't want it, then that's the end of that discussion. And you don't want to be the kind of person who carries negativity of being rejected within you and let it fester inside. This can lead to being overly pressuring which ultimately leads to assault, and that is something you have the power to prevent. Pressuring someone into something they don't want to do is tantamount to assault, and you do not want to have that not just on your conscience, but also on your record. Don't forget: The law applies to you.

Accepting Non-Consent

You might be thinking that accepting her non-consent or rejection is enough and that you'll be able to move on from this and put it behind you. The reality is that it isn't all that easy to be graceful in such situations. Having arrived at the stage of passion and longing through all the effort and charm you brought on and then not having it fulfilled to its natural end can leave one disappointed, depressed, sad, but most importantly, frustrated. Still, as an alpha male, you have a responsibility to accept non-consent without any ifs or buts, and consider this the right thing to do both morally as well as sexually without any reluctance or ill-will.

By ifs or buts, it is implied that you do nothing else at all to even try to start something sexual with her again for the time being. You may have negative thoughts which make you try to salvage the night in one way or the other. This could be by pressuring her to change her mind or even displaying your frustration by lashing out in anger at her. Pestering or intimidating her, or even threatening her physically or emotionally clearly means you're losing the plot and there can be no further salvaging done. It means that you have absolutely no regard for her as a person and individual, and are only interested in gratifying your carnal lusts.

While you may appear to be accepting of her non-consent, there can be several other tiny indicators that make her feel like you aren't completely happy about it, like making her feel stupid or bad, or telling her that she owes it to you. Emotional blackmail can also come into play as you might make her feel guilty that she doesn't care about you enough to make an effort, which would naturally make her feel conflicted about her own self-worth. Negativity can also make you try desperate gambits like intoxicating her with drugs or alcohol to make her more amenable, or even make her prove her worth as a woman.

This isn't you. This isn't the alpha male you are. You're far, far better than this, so take a deep breath and exhale all that negativity out of you. Show her the kind, loving, and caring person you are and respect her desires regardless of how you feel. Being pushy, impatient, and desperate are not the ideal traits of an alpha male.

Pleasing a Woman Sexually

In the best-case scenario, your partner is ready and willing to let you into her body completely, and you're more than ready to become one with her as you engage in the merry dance of sexual intercourse. However, as with all things you've learned throughout your journey as an alpha male, having the best sexual experience isn't something you may necessarily be programmed to do. Sure, you have a biological understanding of how to go about the down and dirty, but there are tons of techniques and methods to make the experience wholly pleasurable not just for you, but more importantly, for her. You're still an alpha male whether you're under the sheets or not, and you must never forget that the goal is to give her the best time, even after the lights go down. That never stops, and it matters even more when it comes to pleasuring her from here to high heaven (Marin, 2019).

Educate Yourself

Yes, sex is an entire field of education when you start to read and research about it. It's not biologically inherent or effortless, and much like any other discipline, it requires time and learning to understand how it works, what works best, and what doesn't. Sex education has a wide variety of topics to read up on, and a plethora of books and reading material to get started. Personal sexual health, different sexual techniques both in your and other cultures and regions, open communication with your partners, different sexual positions and their physical as well as emotional benefits, and even preventing unwanted pregnancies or sexually transmitted infections (STIs). The best part is that learning about it doesn't have to be mundane or too technical, as most of the literature available out there is presented as fun, thrilling, and of course, educational.

Consider Her Needs

Despite educating yourself about the different techniques and nuances involved in sexual activities, it's also important to understand your partner completely in order to have the most mutually satisfying experience. That's the key here: Mutually. It would be downright selfish to put your needs at the forefront and completely ignore what would please her as well. Understand your partner completely, mind, body, and soul. Remember that what works for one woman will not necessarily work for all of them. You've seen that while you were getting to know her as a person, so it's important for you to realize that her sexual needs will also differ from other women. Her body may react differently to the way you touch her vis-a-vis how you used to touch a previous partner.

Of course, you have a great deal of experience with all your past partners and the sexual encounters you've had with them, but that should create a more mature understanding of what to do or not to do in different situations. Never assume that your present partner will react the same way as your previous ones. If the one before liked going down on you and this one doesn't, don't make a direct comparison ever. If you used to do a bit of playful spanking with the previous one, don't go ahead and take that liberty with your present one. You'll only end up antagonizing her if it isn't something she's expecting or used to. Worse still, you may end up hurting her if she has sensitive skin.

Never stop communicating, not even during sex. Talk to her and ask her whether or not she would like it if you did something. The fact that you're in an intimate setting doesn't mean you stop talking to each other. Listen to what she says and doesn't say by keeping track of her body language and non-verbal cues. Watch her breathing and listen to her moans if they sound like she's under pain because of your strokes or your pace. Ask her lovingly if you should go slow or take it easy, or if there's some other position she would prefer.

Be sensitive to her comfort and discomfort, and keep getting her feedback. A good time to do so would be before you begin, so that you can determine just what will please her the most. Even after you've completed the encounter, a bit of pillow talk will help you to manage things in the next one. Tell her what you loved and also find out what she found pleasure in, and also find out what both of you can try the next time around.

Manage Expectations

Remember that biology is an important factor when it comes to having sex, and it differs not just for genders but for people. Medical, emotional, and physical limitations make the experience different from person to person and thus you can't expect all women to operate the same way. Some may be overly sexually active, while others may only open up at their own pace. It's a lot of pressure, particularly on women. Male sexuality is considered the epitome of sexual drive and desire, while female sexuality isn't accorded the same respect. Women are often shamed for not being in the mood or taking too long to be turned on, and face a lot of distress from society as well as men. Being an alpha male, you need to be mindful of the differences between yourself and your partner that aren't just limited to the biological.

Conversely, don't get carried away in your goal to make her feel good about herself. This may create more pressure when it comes to getting her to overcome her fears and get them to enjoy sex. A classic example of this is when you drive her hard to orgasm: You may think you're doing her a favor by realizing her sexual potential, but in reality you're adding tons of pressure on her to perform. Don't make it part of a checklist that you expect her to check off. Orgasm is a pleasurable experience whose only goal is to make her feel incredible. But if your goal is to make her orgasm to feed your ego to know you can make her cream as soon as you push forward, that is not okay.

Understand the fact that people feel differently about sex than you and experience pleasure differently. Getting them in the mood, bringing out sexual arousal, and knowing what they'll like and dislike needs you to be caring, considerate, and empathetic. And of course, ready to communicate.

Communicate about Everything

Being able to readily talk about your desires as well as hers is a fundamental founding pillar for having the best sex. Either one of you may be nervous or timid about talking about sex mostly because of feeling insecure or thinking that it may be gross to talk about it. But the hallmark of being in a great relationship is to be ready and willing to talk about something like sex regardless of how you feel. Sure, it may seem hard in the beginning, but over time both of you will find yourself feeling relieved for having done so.

Self-Confidence Issues

The right kind of communication helps to break down barriers and defenses we put up to protect ourselves from bringing things out in the open. For instance, she may be concerned about her body image and worried about what you might think about her. She's not wrong, though: The insane standards the media bombards women with using photoshopped images and picture-perfect bikini bodies are going to leave her incredibly conscious about not being able to *measure up*. And while you can't really change the way women think about themselves, you can still make them feel more comfortable when the time calls for it. Instead of trying to make her feel good about what she doesn't, compliment the parts of her body you find attractive and pay them special attention. Use your fingers, palms, and lips gently on those areas and tell her how much you're aroused by them.

Avoid Shaming and Verbal Disrespect

Just because she may feel uncomfortable in talking about what's troubling her doesn't give you the right to be verbally disrespectful to her. Shaming a person for being a certain way and being too frigid about discussing things and of course consenting to sex is an expected emotional outburst, but it has disastrous consequences for people who are already too vulnerable about it in the first place. Degrading them by name-calling, slut-shaming, objectifying them just for their physical shortcomings, or not considering their boundaries at all is a negative form of communication and only serves to demean her even more and make you less empathetic in general. Being judgmental will only serve to make you less of an alpha male and make you question your own qualities as a person.

In short, be ready to communicate with your partner in a positive light over just about anything that may be in your mind. Whether it's about any apprehensions you may have about your own position in the relationship, or about how you're perceiving her to be feeling at the moment as you progress along, never hold back about what you're feeling. Sensing your partner's discomfort and not saying anything about it will make her feel as if her needs do not take precedence with you, which couldn't be further from the truth. On the other hand, be careful of how you broach topics that she may find sensitive. Be understanding of her feelings and be prepared to listen to everything she has to say. A key ingredient of empathizing is to not butt in whenever she's trying to put her thoughts forward. You may not even know how much it is taking of her to open up to you in the first place. Similarly, never lash out in anger or rage if you feel slighted by what she tells you. If there's a particular thing she doesn't enjoy in bed but you do, don't take it personally. This isn't about you, it's about how she feels when she's with you. And as an alpha male, you can never let her value be diminished. Ever.

Chapter 7

Developing and

Maintaining Your Alpha-

ness

Staying at the top of your alpha-male game requires constantly working to make sure that you achieve a sense of personal growth with each passing day. Improving yourself on a daily basis with small, calculated, and effective changes can pay dividends and continue to enhance you as a true alpha male for the times. This could be just by inculcating small, everyday habits that you can be proud of, and how they can add value to you as a person as well as an alpha.

Keep in mind that as an alpha male, you are never an unfinished product. You constantly keep improving and looking for areas in your life that you can effectively streamline or even eliminate if it means making you better than you are before. Your daily choices and actions have a major effect on your life that will lead you to reach the ultimate goal of your life, or chart your course in a direction that will deviate from what you desire. Therefore, keep developing and improving yourself in order to clearly see your goals. Motivate yourself toward achieving these goals and craft yourself into a better you in the process.

Continuous Self-Improvement

Working on yourself comes down to a simple choice: Do you want to live with all that life has to offer, or are you content with being a cog in the machine? Does that sound familiar? Of course it does, it's the beta approach to thinking. Now you're probably wondering why you're having a beta thought now that you've reached alpha-male status, until it hits you that retaining your alpha-ness will require a lot more effort than gaining it. A beta will always be someone with a fixed mindset who remains happy with what he has, thus he won't aim for anything greater or higher to improve his circumstances. To a beta, people are how they are right out of the box and may not be worth changing or find it difficult to gain new talents, which means they'll only aim for whatever is in their comfort zone (*23 Self Improvement Exercises to Transform Your Life*, 2018).

Is that the kind of person you are? Of course not, far from it. That is what the whole point of all these pages has been. Having a mindset that prioritizes self-growth and improvement means that you will keep learning and receiving an education from anywhere and everywhere. This will help you to enhance and build your intelligence and capabilities so long as you put in the required effort and hard work, as well as remain patient and persistent. As an alpha, you'll have to constantly develop and sculpt your identity and personality not just as a priority, but as a rule to live by through the rest of your life. This is the only way you'll be able to realize your goals and achieve success in life, which is only possible through rigorous self-discipline.

Improving Yourself Mentally

Like the struggles you made to reach your current state, remaining an alpha male means keeping up with the times and constantly evolving to remain modern and relevant. This requires continuously educating yourself about the latest trends, the things people find interesting, and even using ideas from the past to bring about a kind of revolution. There's an abundance of literature available on all sorts of ways and habits for every situation, so reading more books is a definite educational experience. Taking even 20 to 30 minutes of your day to read a book about a certain topic will not only be enriching, but also an eye-opening experience. Whether it's hardcovers or paperbacks, blogs or articles, the written word provides tons of insights that effectively contribute to your personality and intelligence.

Regular meditation also helps to relax your mind and clear your thoughts. Having some time to yourself to think about your life and where you are in it, as well as where you'd like to be, will be all the more soothing when you're in an environment of calm and peace without any pressure. Seeking out yourself in quiet meditation and contemplation allows you to determine your purpose in life as well as face your fears. Mentally charting out the path you must take and marking out the challenges that come in between help you to clearly identify what you need to do next and set realistic targets for yourself to overcome as time goes by.

Improving Yourself Physically

Never stay in one place for too long. Getting into the ideal physical shape may have gotten you to be the alpha male you wanted to be, but keeping yourself in shape is doubly challenging. Keep at your exercise routine with discipline and rigor, and never fall for laziness or procrastination. Aside from regular exercise, exert yourself physically in other outdoor activities such as hiking and rock climbing. These will also get you to learn new skills as you expand your horizons and add more versatility to your repertoire.

Speaking of discipline, don't forget about your diet and eating right. Being mindful of what you eat and how you eat it is essential as you not only retain your alpha-male shape, but also keep yourself medically fit. Eating in portions and avoiding random snacks or overeating help you to manage your digestion and blood circulation, as well as improve your overall eating experience. Create a proper routine of meal times and breaks, and stick by it like glue. Make sure to eat just right in order to have the energy you need for your physical, and even sexual, excursions. Don't forget your water intake, either.

Improving Yourself Emotionally

Your emotional well-being is just as important as either your physical or mental well-being, if not more. Though it may appear to be a bit self-indulgent, caring for your own emotional state is crucial when it comes to dealing with the negative vibes that may surround us everywhere. Whether it's work or the state of current affairs, we can slowly feel ourselves getting overwhelmed due to stress and exhaustion. This can result in being lax in worrying about our own welfare and the negativity can have toxic effects on us overall, physically, mentally, and emotionally.

Therefore, don't forget to show a little bit of tender loving care, or TLC, to yourself as well. Destressing and forgetting about all the woes in life and all that's wrong with the world will help you to break away from the pressures of society and avoid being pulled in by its tentacles' vicious grip. An emotionally healthy you is essential if you want your mental and physical self to be at the top of their game, and make you take on the challenges that life throws at you. Take some time out of your schedule every day to highlight all the things that are going well for you. This will help you feel a lot better about yourself and let you remember and appreciate all that you have instead of worrying about everything else.

Understanding Your Lifestyle

Attaining alpha-male status is one thing, but remember that nothing lasts forever. Never forget that your time on Earth is limited, so live every day with that knowledge and be at peace with it. That means making every day count and not wasting it on irrelevancies. Being proactive with our life and the elements that make it worth living is a lot more important. Making your life comfortable by being responsible for ourselves and the people in our lives should be a priority, as should be leaving your mark. As each day could be your last, never shy away from realizing your true potential. Be someone who sets a trend instead of just a follower. Be someone others will look up to and be inspired by, but never forget to be inspired yourself.

Acting Responsibly

It's a duty of every alpha male to live with a sense of responsibility to himself and the people who depend on him. Whether you're single, in a relationship, fishing the seas, or even married with children, your choices will determine the kind of lifestyle you'll be able to afford. Focus on the essentials and make sure that the lights in your house stay on and the kitchen is fully stocked—not to mention that you should have something set aside for a rainy day or in case you ever face something unexpected that you weren't able to control. In any case, an alpha male does his best to never be unprepared. Naturally, one can't prepare for everything, but at least you'll be in a better position to tackle it when the time comes.

This doesn't just apply to financial risks, but even to dealing with other people—especially women. Tempting and engaging a total stranger for future liaisons is one thing, but forgetting to have proper protection when the clothes come off is another. Therefore, use common sense and intelligence before taking any sort of risk.

Managing Your Money

Whether or not you're made of money, you should always treat it as an attribute of yourself that requires stern supervision. Keeping track of your savings and expenses shows you to be prudent and responsible, and an example that will inspire others to do the same. Make proper budgets either mentally or on paper, and take complete control of your finances. Every dollar matters, and whatever you save today can be used to create more comfort for yourself and the people who depend on you.

Never forget that it's your money, and the way you spend it shows your level of discipline and intelligence. The attitude of an alpha male must always be that "money is no object," but they should have the money to begin with. Spending needlessly on things that don't add value to you as a person, or expenses are all flash and no substance, is only indicative of someone who doesn't think ahead and is only living for the moment. Flashy cars, expensive watches, and frivolous vacations are just irresponsible spending that diminish in value immediately and lead to bankruptcy at the worst. To an alpha, hard work, dedication, prudent saving, and investing is the best way to be more responsible with money.

Constantly Evolving

Once you've reached the zenith of your current social status, you may feel things moving slowly or not at all, which is a sure sign of redundancy and stagnation. In the case of the alpha male, this state will choke the life out of him and smother his potential. Thus it is necessary to keep moving forward and explore one new horizon after another. If you feel that your current social circle isn't as stimulating you as you'd like, don't sweat moving on to find new social groups. This allows you to learn—and be inspired by—new things that you were previously unaware of and create new goals for yourself that allow you to push yourself further and test your limits. Be in tune with your energy and realize when you feel it waning. Break out of the vicious cycle you've put yourself in and strive for new challenges to make you feel alive.

Taking Pride

It is a huge achievement that you've created constant and lasting changes in yourself and your lifestyle that will make you the envy of the world. So it doesn't hurt at all to be able to look at yourself in the mirror with a sense of pride and appreciation for the man you are now versus the man you were before. It also helps to take stock of your present position to understand not just how far you've come along in your journey, but how far ahead you can still go.

In order to measure just how well you're progressing in your quest to become the best version of yourself, keep one thing absolutely clear: Don't be apprehensive of what you want to achieve. By realizing that the world is your oyster as far as gaining new skills or talents is concerned, you won't be limiting your ambitions to certain niche areas that appeal to you. Conversely, you don't even want to try out things that don't suit your personality or abilities as well, not yet anyways—which means you shouldn't go ahead and enlist yourself in professional bungee jumping just because you feel like pushing yourself further.

So monitor your progress, and highlight the milestones you achieve along the way. Appreciate your achievements, but don't just sit on your laurels.

Create a Bucket List

No, not that bucket list—though if you think about it, an alpha male doesn't stop gaining and developing as if they've achieved everything they could. It certainly doesn't mean that they can die in peace, but rather they can look forward to the things that they would still like to accomplish. And a bucket list with things to do before you die may not sound like the ideal way to go about it, but the way it is normally made should set things in perspective for you.

The true goal of a bucket list is and always has been to accomplish goals in your life that you've forever ignored and would like to accomplish before you die. This is equally divided into various areas that may comprise learning new skills, traveling to uncharted territory, gaining new insights and education, and transforming yourself accordingly. Think about it. When was the last time you thought of doing something daring like skydiving or flying around the world in a solar plane? Or how many exotic locations deep in the darkest regions of the Amazon jungle have you always dreamed of exploring? Haven't you always been fascinated by discovering life underneath the ocean bed, or even thought about wanting to play a musical instrument with perfection?

With a bucket list, you'll be able to keep track of the things you would have otherwise never gotten around to. It will help you to monitor how much you're growing with each new experience and help you discover whole new vistas to immerse yourself in.

Write About Your Progress

In the current age of blogs and online motivational videos, most people end up living the experiences of other people rather than themselves. If our focus is completely toward other people's achievements, where does that leave us and our own achievements? Sure, these experiences should be an inspiration for us to do the same. We mostly find ourselves contemplating what value addition they would put in ourselves rather than realizing its true potential. Writing about our own growth and experiences can be an eye opener into your life as if someone else were reading you as a book. In the past, writing journals and notes about one's experiences was a healthy habit that logged their journeys not just for posterity, but also to look back at and gain insights they may have missed before.

Even leaders, professionals, statesmen and industry leaders have maintained their own memoirs or journals to learn valuable lessons as well as provide lessons to others who may chance upon their pages. Military leaders, naval captains, officers, and the like are required to keep logs of their exploits. These aren't just technical reports that provide details into their missions, but also look into their own conscience whenever they have been weighted by difficult choices. Documenting their decision making and inner conflicts provides them with knowledge and foresight for such situations in the future.

So as an alpha male, don't dismiss the power of writing a journal. Knowing your own motivations rather than those coming from others will help you to lay out goals for the future and measure how well you're able to tackle certain ones immediately, while saving the ones you feel you can accomplish in the due course of time for later.

Manage Your Time Well

Never forget that your time on the earth is limited, and all your goals will require you to take time out for working on them, let alone achieving them. More often than not, people start off working on a goal but aren't able to devote enough time to it to see any kind of realistic and tangible changes. The end result is that they become disappointed and disillusioned with the whole goal, and this negative energy may spill over into achieving all the other goals. For instance, learning a new language requires not just taking classes and speaking with others, but also talking to yourself and in other settings where the language isn't necessarily used. In short, it needs your time that you use in other pursuits to make you think in the language in order to better understand it and gain fluency as well as command over it.

On the other hand, you may also have a great chunk of free time on your hand and not know exactly what to do with it. Here's one thing that you should *never* do, though: Squander it. Watching the odd TV show for maybe an hour a day is one thing, but aiming to binge-watch an entire series of 10 seasons in the course of a few days is basically flushing all your time away down the toilet. Make proper use of your time and develop habits to effectively assign the right amount of time for your goals. Estimate just how much time you need to devote to achieve a certain goal and then make a time table to do nothing but pursue that goal within that time frame only. You can even do this every morning while you're having breakfast, or every night before you go to sleep. Mentally sort through the most important tasks that lay ahead of you, and chart out a course of how you'll accomplish them.

Self-Discipline

Elbert Hubbard once defined self-discipline as "the ability to do what you have to do, when you have to do it, whether you feel like it or not." (Logue, 2019)

Creating discipline in your life and habits makes living life a lot easier as well as efficient. It also fosters healthy and positive habits, as well as bringing about positive changes in your lifestyle. The more rigorous you are with your self-discipline, the better it will be to unlock your true potential and achieve your goals.

Living your life with a sense of discipline might seem daunting at times, so it's important to understand just how life would be if you let your routines and habits slip. For one thing, having a lackadaisical approach in one aspect of life will automatically spread out to cover actually meaningful goals that you are aiming to achieve. Before you know it, you may end up accepting yourself to just go with the flow and stop worrying about things as if they were insignificant to you. But ask yourself this: Would you be better off living life as if you were dead?

Your self-discipline lets you be surrounded by healthy and positive energy, and that in turn leads you to create positive and effective habits. These habits will then spread into the rest of your life and let you create your own happiness wherever you can find it. And yes, while we're on the subject, happiness isn't that easy to achieve. It requires hard work, sacrifice, and above all, a desire to continuously improve. Happiness can only be achieved once you're ready to move on from what you were to what you want to be. It will also help to eliminate all the excuses you come up with that hinder your proactivity.

Build Self-Discipline

It's actually rather easy to come up with excuses to stray away from being self-disciplined. All it takes is simply not wanting to do what needs to be done in order to get the most out of life. Regardless of whatever it is you want to achieve out of life, the reality is that no one else is going to do it for you. Whether it's making a ton of money, getting the alpha-male physique you crave, or making a move with the beautiful woman at the bar, no one else is going to hold your hand and get it for you. Once you become sufficiently independent and start to choose what's best for your life, you become responsible for yourself and your own choices. Work, relationships, neighborhoods, diets—it all comes down to you.

"The biggest enemy to success," according to Brian Tracy, "is the path of least resistance" (Tracy, 2013). You'll never find true happiness or success if you opt for taking the easy way out. Hard work, diligence, and sacrifice are the only ways one can achieve success in any aspect of life. Be responsible for your life. No one else is going to let you take the reins to their life, will they? Create a clear goal or goals and proper plans to get what it is out of life. Then work hard and persistently to put those plans into action and realize your goals. Revise and go over your goals every day and visualize just how wonderful the outcome will be. Conversely, also map out any expected setbacks so that you'll be ready for them when the time comes. Commit yourself to being successful, and there is nothing you can't achieve. It may not be today or tomorrow, but it will happen for sure.

Lack of Discipline

You might be asking just how much of a difference can self-discipline actually make in your life. Take stock of your habits and ask yourself some simple yet poignant questions. Have you ever left a bookmark halfway through a book and never opened it up again? Have you ever bought a home workout DVD or an indoor spinning machine with the aim to get in better shape, but abandoned the idea because you thought you could do it some other time? Have you ever made New Year's resolutions to get rid of a habit, but never really followed through? Or thought of starting your own business? Or getting new furniture? Or even getting something repaired that keeps wearing down? Why do you think that is?

The answer is really simple: A lack of self-discipline. The inability to actually follow through on all the mental plans you make and lay out with an aim to get from one point to another, but never truly take off. It may start from small things, sure, but when you look at it from a broader perspective, you can see just where you might have let your life slip away from your control.

There are several reasons why we find ourselves stuck in a rut of mundaneness at times. We begin to identify ourselves as a slob or a couch potato or the one who knows we don't have our lives under control and laugh out loud with our friends about it. We take something as counterproductive as laziness in our stride, making it a part of our identity. Of course, as we reach adulthood, we find ourselves making our own mark by living by no one else's rules. With the exception of who signs our paychecks, we believe we're our own masters and left to our own devices, so we can sleep late and wear the same clothes for a week without feeling any remorse or guilt.

Conclusion

Remove all the buts and excuses from your life. Don't assign blame for your shortcomings on something else. Take full responsibility for your actions, or inactions in this case, as this is how you'll be able to cultivate your sense of self-discipline effectively. Continuing to make excuses and looking for whatever it is that may be responsible will keep you from achieving your goals. Here's one way to ensure this: Remove temptations. Do away with anything and everything from your environment that tempts you to stray away from your goals. It could be the leftover pizza that could ruin your diet, or that TV series you haven't finished binge-watching yet. Once you eliminate those temptations, you reassert your self-control and become more self-disciplined.

Be more organized, whether it's your sock drawer or your overall physical space. Once you've organized it to perfection and know where everything is, your mind is de-stressed, relaxed, and focused, considering that our strength of will can only cope with so much throughout the day. Practicing healthy activities such as joy, peace, love and optimism will make you good at them, but what you don't realize is that practicing negative and toxic activities such as anger, rage, complaining, and fear will also make you good at them as well. This will lead you to an existence that is nothing more than a vicious cycle and is largely of your own making.

Much like the muscles in your body, your self-discipline requires a similar exercise routine that requires you to constantly push ahead. When you're exercising your body, you start from a base weight capacity and then add more when you feel yourself getting stronger and ready to take on more. The same is the case with your self-discipline, as you start from a position of relative laziness and low resolve which you need to enhance with each little obstacle. Controlling your eating habits, getting a grip on your finances, organizing your living space and keeping it organized, taking more responsibilities in and around the house—all of these areas let you build your discipline one step at a time and exert more self-control over areas that you previously had no grip on. Once you master control over one area, you can take on the next and the next and so on steadily and with greater efficiency. Don't overdo it, though, as tackling everything at once in a blind rage will only exhaust you. Start with something small and gradually move on to the next area that could use more self-discipline. Eventually, you'll be proud of all the things you now have a handle on.

Above all else, keep going and never stop. Whether it's failure or adversity, never stop pushing forward. Live to fight another day and learn from your mistakes. Hard work and perseverance are going to get you through, and that is why it becomes something special when you finally achieve it. If it were supposed to be easy, anybody could do it. But it isn't, and only you—the alpha male—wants it badly enough.

Self-Worth Affirmations

❖ I am unique. I feel good about being alive and being me.

❖ Life is fun and rewarding.

❖ Amazing opportunities exist for me in every aspect of my life.

❖ There are no such things as problems, only opportunities.

❖ I love challenges; they bring out the best in me.

❖ I replace "I must", "I should" and "I have to" with "I choose". (try it with something you think you have to do, and replace must with choose... notice the difference?)

❖ I choose to be happy right now. I love my life.

❖ I appreciate everything I have. I live in joy.

❖ I am courageous. I am willing to act in spite of any fear.

❖ I am positive and optimistic. I believe things will always work out for the best.

❖ It's easy to make friends. I attract positive and kind people into my life.

❖ It's easy to meet people. I create positive and supportive relationships.

❖ I am a powerful creator. I create the life I want.

❖ I am OK as I am. I accept and love myself.

❖ I am confident. I trust myself.

❖ I am successful right now.

❖ I am passionate. I am outrageously enthusiastic and inspire others.

❖ I am calm and peaceful.

❖ I have unlimited power at my disposal.

❖ I am optimistic. I believe things will always work out for the best.

❖ I am kind and loving. I am compassionate and truly care for others.

❖ I am focused and persistent. I will never quit.

❖ I am energetic and enthusiastic. Confidence is my second nature.

❖ I treat everyone with kindness and respect.

❖ I inhale confidence and exhale fear.

❖ I am flexible. I adapt to change quickly.

❖ I have integrity. I am totally reliable. I do what I say.

❖ I am competent, smart and able.

❖ I believe in myself,

❖ I recognize the many good qualities I have.

❖ I see the best in other people.

- ❖ I surround myself with people who bring out the best in me.

- ❖ I let go of negative thoughts and feelings about myself.

- ❖ I love who I have become.

- ❖ I am always growing and developing.

- ❖ My opinions resonate with who I am.

- ❖ I am congruent in everything I say and do.

- ❖ I deserve to be happy and successful

- ❖ I have the power to change myself

- ❖ I can forgive and understand others and their motives

❖ I can make my own choices and decisions

❖ I am free to choose to live as I wish and to give priority to my desires

❖ I can choose happiness whenever I wish no matter what my circumstances

❖ I am flexible and open to change in every aspect of my life

❖ I act with confidence having a general plan and accept plans are open to alteration

❖ It is enough to have done my best

❖ I deserve to be loved

❖ I have high self-esteem

- ❖ I love and respect myself.

- ❖ I am a great person.

- ❖ I respect myself deeply.

- ❖ My thoughts and opinions are valuable.

- ❖ I am confident that I can achieve anything.

- ❖ I have something special to offer the world.

- ❖ Others like and respect me.

- ❖ I am a wonderful human being I feel great about myself and my life.

- ❖ I am worthy of having high self-esteem.

❖ I believe in myself.

❖ I deserve to feel good about myself.

❖ I know I can achieve anything.

❖ Having respect for myself helps others to like and respect me.

❖ Feeling good about myself is normal for me.

❖ Improving my self-esteem is very important.

❖ Being confident in myself comes naturally to me.

❖ Liking and respecting myself is easy.

❖ Speaking my mind with confidence is something I just naturally do.

❖ Each day I notice I am more self-discipline.

❖ I enjoy being self-disciplined.

❖ I am doing the best I can with the knowledge and experience I have obtained so far.

❖ It's OK to make mistakes. They are opportunities to learn.

❖ I always follow through on my promises.

❖ I treat others with kindness and respect.

❖ I see myself with kind eyes.

❖ I am a unique and a very special person.

❖ I love myself more each day.

- ❖ I am willing to change.

- ❖ I approve of myself.

- ❖ I care about myself.

- ❖ I am a child of God.

- ❖ My work gives me pleasure.

- ❖ I give praise freely.

- ❖ I am respected by others.

- ❖ I rejoice in my uniqueness.

- ❖ I attract praise.

- ❖ I deserve good in my life.

❖ I appreciate myself.

❖ Each day I am becoming more self-confident.

"ALL THAT WE ARE IS THE RESULT OF WHAT WE HAVE THOUGHT"

Buddha

ALPHA MALE DATING
The Essential Playbook

Single → Engaged → Married (If You Want).
Love Hypnosis, Law of Attraction,
Art of Seduction, Intimacy in Bed.
Attract Women as an Irresistible Alpha Man.

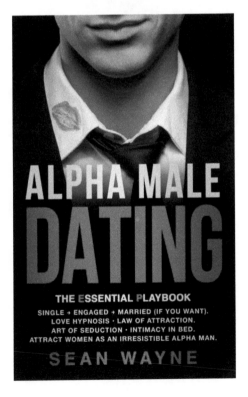

ALPHA MALE
the 7 Laws of POWER
**Mindset & Psychology of Success.
Manipulation, Persuasion, NLP Secrets.
Analyze & Influence Anyone.
Hypnosis Mastery • Emotional Intelligence.
Win as a Real Alpha Man.**

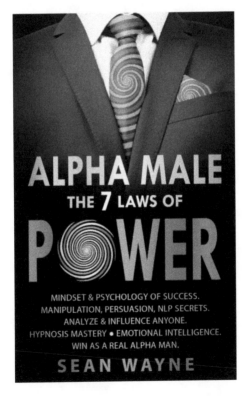

SUPREME ALPHA MALE BIBLE
The 1ne
Empath & Psychic Abilities Power.
Success Mindset, Psychology, Confidence.
Win Friends & Influence People.
Hypnosis, Body Language, Atomic Habits.
Dating: The Secret.

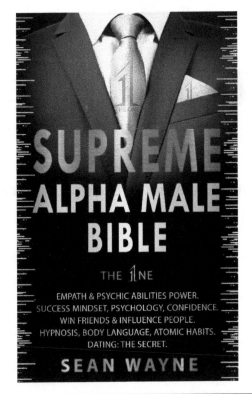

I Would Appreciate It if You Left a
Review,
It's Very Important.

 SEAN WAYNE

mr.sean.wayne.author@gmail.com